ECONOMICS

A Complete Course

Question and Revision Book

Dan Moynihan • Brian Titley

Third Edition

OXFORD

UNIVERSITY PRESS

OXFORD
UNIVERSITY PRESS

Great Clarendon Street, Oxford OX2 6DP

Oxford University Press is a department of the University of Oxford.
It furthers the University's objective of excellence in research,
scholarship, and education by publishing worldwide in

Oxford New York

Auckland Cape Town Dar es Salaam Hong Kong Karachi
Kuala Lumpur Madrid Melbourne Mexico City Nairobi
New Delhi Shanghai Taipei Toronto

With offices in

Argentina Austria Brazil Chile Czech Republic France Greece
Guatemala Hungary Italy Japan South Korea Poland Portugal
Singapore Switzerland Thailand Turkey Ukraine Vietnam

Oxford is a registered trade mark of Oxford University Press
in the UK and in certain other countries

British Library Cataloguing in Publication Data

Data available

ISBN: 978 0 19 913436 6

10

Typeset by Tech-Set Ltd, Gateshead, Tyne and Wear

Printed in China

Acknowledgements

The authors and publishers thank the following for permission to use
photographs: p 12 Corbis UK Ltd (left & centre), Format Photographers (right);
p 13 Corbis UK Ltd. Additional photography by Chris Honeywell and OUP ©.

Contents

Chapter 1 | The Economic Problem

The resources available worldwide to produce the goods and services that we need and want are scarce compared to the unlimited wants of people. This is the central problem of economics. That is there is **scarcity**.

Because of scarcity, people must choose which wants they will satisfy because they cannot satisfy them all. Choice is necessary because scarce resources can be used in many different ways to make many different goods and services. For example, an area of land can be used to build houses or used as an industrial site, but it cannot be used for both. Similarly, when a person gets a job as a builder they cannot at the same time be a bank clerk. Thus people, nations and the world must choose how scarce resources are used; they must choose which goods and services to make because they cannot make everything that they want.

Choosing between goods and services involves a cost. The real cost of choosing one thing and not another is known as the **opportunity cost**. This measures the benefit that could have been had from the next best alternative gone without. For example, when using a piece of land to build and industrial site people are going without the houses that may have been built there instead.

Economics attempts to increase people's choice. It involves advising how best to use the scarce resources that we have in order to make goods and services to satisfy as many wants as possible.

MULTIPLE CHOICE

1 Which of the following is not included in the study of economics?

   A Scarce resources
   B Choice
   C The satisfaction of wants
   D What people should buy
   E Opportunity cost

2 Which of the following could be classed as a value judgement?

   1 The Government should tax the poor more.
   2 Unemployment is rising.
   3 Unemployment is too high.
   4 More money should be given to poorer countries.

   A All of the above
   B 1 only
   C 1, 3 and 4
   D 1 and 3 only
   E None of the above

3 Which of the following could be classed as a free good?

   A Air
   B Land
   C Television programmes
   D Bank loans
   E Christmas presents

4 Which of the following statements would be of most interest to a person who studies economics?

   A Pensions should be raised.
   B The Government should create more jobs.
   C Arsenal deserve to win the Premiership.
   D We should be more concerned with rising prices than with unemployment.
   E Prices are rising faster than last year.

(continued)

5 The opportunity cost of a good is:

  A The total cost of the good.
  B What goods can be sold for.
  C How much it is worth to its owner.
  D The other goods which have been foregone
  E The cost of producing one more of the good.

6 A new dam is built in Turkey to provide hydroelectric power and a water supply. What is the opportunity cost to the economy of building the dam?

  A The cost to households and businesses of consuming the water supply
  B The benefits foregone from other uses of the money used to pay for the dam
  C The cost of borrowing the money by the Turkish Government to pay for the dam
  D The cost to consumers of using hydroelectric power
  E The money used to pay for the construction and running of the dam

7 The total amount of goods and services produced in any country will be:

  A Determined by nature and not controlled by humans.
  B Unlimited.
  C Just enough to satisfy people's wants.
  D Less than people want.
  E Not produced by scarce resources.

8 A firm can produce a number of possible combinations of two goods. It can either produce 500 of good x and 300 of good y, or 600 x and 250 y. What is the opportunity of producing the extra 100 of good x?

  A 100 y
  B 250 y
  C Nothing
  D 50 y
  E The extra wages they pay workers.

DATA RESPONSE 1

Buddha loses his serenity to a theme park

For more than 2000 years the Nepali village of Lumbini – birthplace of Buddha – has been an oasis of tranquillity and spirituality. But if Nepal's new government has its way the calm of Lumbini, one of the four holiest places in Buddhism, will be shattered. In its 'masterplan' 1000 tourists a day will file through a huge $60 million complex of museums, a 'Lord Buddha' wildlife sanctuary and a sculpture park. Up to 12 big hotels will be built, and a new airport and roads are planned. An entrance fee may be charged.

The plans have generated controversy in Nepal and the global Buddhist community. One senior Nepali Buddhist monk says Lumbini risks being a 'theme-park'. Another claims its 'precious calm' will be lost. Local Muslims also fear that their own sites of worship will be affected and some Nepali environmentalists say that precious habitats for wildlife could be threatened. They argue the money would be better spent on new schools, hospitals and transport links in the most deprived areas of the country.

But many Nepalis support the plan. The country is still one of the poorest in the world, and tourism one of its biggest industries. 'We all want Lumbini to be as developed as possible to attract tourists,' said Serish Pradsan, editor of the current affairs magazine Explore Nepal in the capital Kathmandu. 'We need to transform the area into a big, bustling tourist centre.'

Adapted from *The Guardian*, 5.9.1999

1 Define opportunity cost and explain how the above article can be used to illustrate opportunity cost. (6 marks)

2 Why do you think the Government of Nepal is involved in the decision to develop the land at Lumbini? (4 marks)

3 What are the possible benefits to the economy of Nepal of the proposed development? (4 marks)

4 You have been appointed as a consultant to a pressure group in Nepal. They have asked you to prepare a report comparing the plans for Lumbini with alternative proposals to spend an extra $60 million on new schools and hospitals. Suggest what information you would need to help you produce your report, and to make a recommendation on the best use of the money. (8 marks)

Chapter 2 — The Language of Economics

In order to study economics it is necessary to understand the language of economists. The following is a list of definitions of some of the key words in economics.

An **economy** is any area in which people make or produce goods and services from scarce resources. This area can be of any size. Economists often talk of regions within a country as local economies, a country as a national economy and all countries in the world as the world economy.

Production is any activity designed to satisfy people's wants; it involves the making and selling of goods and services. The using up of these goods and services to satisfy our wants is known as **consumption**.

All the producers and consumers of a particular good of service make up its **market**. A market could be local, national or international depending on the nature of the goods or service and the number of people who want it.

Resources are known as **factors of production** and are used to produce goods and services. **Land** refers to all natural resources, **labour** to human effort, and **capital** to man-made resources such as machines. **Entrepreneurs** are the people who combine resources in a firm and take the risks and decisions necessary to help that firm run successfully.

Resources can be used to produce **consumer goods** to satisfy consumer wants or **capital goods**, like machines and buildings, that help produce other goods and services. The buying of capital goods by producers is known as **investment**.

Sometimes the Government or **public sector** will provide goods and services because they feel everyone deserves them whether they can pay for them or not. Examples of such **merit goods** are health care and education.

They may also provide goods and services from which everyone can benefit but no private firm would be able to charge for, because no one would pay for their use. Examples of such **public goods** are street-lighting, defence, law and order.

Unless resources are freely available, firms will pay the owners of land, labour and capital to use them to produce goods and services. For example, labour is paid wages. Economists will also examine factor payments in terms of opportunity cost, or how much a factor earns compared to the payment it would receive in its next best use.

The **transfer earnings** of a factor of production are how much that factor could earn in its next best use. For example, an actor might earn £100 000 per year. If he were not an actor he might be a carpenter earning £15 000 per year. £15 000 per year is the actor's transfer earnings.

Economic rent is the amount of money that a factor of production earns over and above its transfer earnings. In the example above the actor has an economic rent of £85 000 per year. It is possible for all of the factors of production to receive transfer earnings and economic rent.

MULTIPLE CHOICE

1 In the study of economics, resources are also known as:

   A Workers and machines.
   B Raw materials.
   C The output from production
   D Factors of production.
   E Profits.

2 Production can be defined as:

   A Any activity that turns raw materials into finished goods.
   B Any activity that makes and sells goods and services.
   C Any activity that is designed to satisfy wants.
   D Any activity that makes a profit.
   E Any activity that uses resources.

3 Which of the following is a consumer durable good?

   A Apples
   B A doctor
   C Alcohol
   D Detergent
   E A radio

4 An essential feature of a public good is:

   A It is provided by a government.
   B It is provided by private firms.
   C It satisfies some consumer wants.
   D Its consumption cannot be confined to those who pay for it.
   E It involves high production costs and so must be paid for from taxes.

5 In economics, economic rent means:

   A The payment made to landowners.
   B The payment made to use housing accommodation.
   C The amount a factor of production can earn over and above its transfer earnings.
   D The total amount a factor of production can earn.
   E The payment for risk.

6 Which of the following would be classed as capital?

   A Money
   B A television
   C Minerals
   D Shoes
   E An office complex

7 A market consists of:

   A A collection of stalls.
   B All the people wanting to make and sell products.
   C All the producers and consumers of a particular product.
   D A place where money is exchanged for goods and services.
   E A place where people buy products.

8 Which of the following is investment in the economic sense?

   A A bank deposit account
   B Buying a house
   C Building a new factory
   D Buying gold and silver
   E Saving money

9 An entrepreneur is someone who:

   A Owns a factory.
   B Takes the risks and decisions necessary to organize resources.
   C Is a talented worker.
   D Is a supervisor in charge of workers.
   E Is a producer.

10 What are the transfer earnings of a factor of production currently earning £12 500 per year with a next best use that would pay £6750 per year?

   A £6750
   B £12 500
   C £19 250
   D £5750
   E £8750

1 Look at the pictures above. Which of the commodities displayed
   can be classed as:
   a Non-durable consumer goods?
   b Durable consumer goods?
   c Capital goods? (6 marks)

2 Factors of production are combined by entrepreneurs to produce
   goods and services. Classify the following list of factors as:
   a Land   **b** Capital   **c** Labour   (6 marks)

Sheep	Water	Tractor driver
Wood	Screwdriver	Clothes designer
Bank clerk	Blast furnace	Pencil
Juggernaut	Desk-top computer	
Oil	Office block	

3 Give two examples, in each case, of goods and services provided by:
   a The private sector.
   b The public sector. (4 marks)

4 Explain two reasons why the public sector in an economy may
   provide some goods and services. (4 marks)

Chapter 3

Economic Systems

The central economic problem arises because resources are scarce relative to unlimited wants. Choosing which wants to satisfy therefore involves deciding what to produce, how much of each good and service to produce and for whom to produce. This is known as the problem of **resource allocation**.

Every society or country must solve the three problems involved in satisfying wants. Exactly how a society or country decides what, how and for whom to produce is called its **economic system**. There are many different types of economic system.

In a **market economic system** the decisions of producers and consumers solve the problems of what, how and for whom to produce. Producers make those goods and services which give the most profit. Consumers secure as many goods and services as their incomes permit.

In a **planned economic system** decisions about what to produce, how to produce and for whom to produce are made by the government. Planners employed by the government decide exactly how to use scarce resources often with the intention of producing those goods and services they think all their people need and want. They may also try to share them out more equally among their population.

In a **mixed economic system** government planning is combined with the use of the free market to determine resource allocation.

While some economies have managed to develop into rich and powerful nations whose populations enjoy a wide range of goods and services, many other economies are much less well developed. A **less developed country** (LDC) is normally characterized by a generally poor population living in poor housing, receiving little or no education, with a low life expectancy and no access to clean water or the modern conveniences of shops and transport. People in such countries often have very little choice and many rely on aid from more developed economies to try to improve their position.

MULTIPLE CHOICE

1 The basic economic problem faced by all economies is:
   A Rising prices.
   B Unemployment.
   C Scarcity of resources.
   D Pollution.
   E Poor relations between managers and workers.

2 The problem of what to produce in a planned economy is solved mainly by:
   A Consumers.

B The profit motive.
C Market forces.
D Government directives.
E Traditional methods.

3 A mixed economy is one that has:
   A Large and small firms.
   B Farms and factories.
   C A public and a private sector.
   D Capital and consumer goods.
   E Goods and services.

(continued)

4   In a free market economy the price mechanism:

A   Helps the Government to provide services.
B   Measures the total value of wealth.
C   Allows consumers to work out how much they have spent.
D   Allocate scarce resources.
E   Makes profits for firms.

5   During the 1990s the economies of Eastern Europe changed from planned economies to market economic systems. Which of the following best describes the change that took place?

A   More centralised government planning to allocate resources
B   Fewer price controls
C   Increased dependence on the price mechanism to allocate resources
D   More privately owned firms
E   Increased resource unemployment

6   A less developed country may have all the following characteristics *except*:

A   A poor education system.
B   A low level of income.
C   Poor sanitation and water supplies.
D   A high birth rate.
E   A high level of capital investment.

7   Which of the following is an advantage claimed for the market economic system?

A   It responds quickly to consumer wants.
B   It provides public goods.
C   Unemployment can rise rapidly.
D   It ensures a high standard of living for all.
E   It relies on traditional methods of production.

8   Which of the following is more likely to occur in a mixed economy than a planned economy?

A   Full employment
B   Higher taxation
C   Improved standard of living
D   A greater variety of goods and services
E   Lower prices

DATA RESPONSE 1

CHINA AGREES TO FREE TRADE

Businesses in the West were gearing up this week for a huge export drive to China after six days of talks between Beijing and Washington paved the way for the full opening up of the world's largest potential consumer market.

China's leaders agreed to a package of trade measures that will provide opportunities for the West's banks, insurers, farmers, internet companies and film-makers.

Beijing's concessions – which will cement the 20-year transition from a command economy to a mixed market economy – were enough to win US support for China's membership of the World Trade Organisation, the Geneva-based body that polices the global trading system.

The accord ends 13 years of negotiations, and is seen as setting the seal on China's transformation into a free-market economy.

It has also raised hopes of an influx of foreign investment, which has been declining recently.

Access to China's 1.2bn consumers could boost Western exports by $21bn a year, according to the Institute of International Economics in Washington. Those sectors likely to benefit most will be hi-tech companies, Wall Street, telecommunications firms and farmers, who will be able to get access to China's heavily protected agricultural market.

The deal gives the Chinese prime minister a mandate to push ahead with economic reforms. These include privatising loss-making state enterprises and forcing workers to pay market rents for previously subsidised housing.

Adapted from *The Guardian*, 17.11.1999

1 Contrast how resources are allocated in a command, or planned, economy and a market economy. (8 marks)

2 China is adopting a mixed economic system. Discuss why this might be preferable to a market or command economy. (8 marks)

3 With the use of a diagram, explain what may now happen in China if
 a consumer demand for a product rises,
 b the cost of producing it falls. (4 marks)

4 Explain how international trade can benefit China. (4 marks)

5 Explain the meaning of the statement underlined in the article. (4 marks)

Six key states push world to 9bn people

The world's population will grow from 6.1billion today to about 9.3 billion by 2050, according to a UN report published yesterday.

It estimates that the world's population is growing by 1.2% annually, or 77 m people, and six countries account for half the increase: India, China, Pakistan, Nigeria, Bangladesh and Indonesia.

The population division of the UN department of economic and social affairs points to growing imbalance between developed and developing countries, the population growth concentrated overwhelmingly in those countries least able to support it. The 48 least developed countries are expected to nearly triple their population, from 658 m to 1.8 bn.

Adapted from *The Guardian*, 1.3.2001

1 Identify and explain the main characteristics of a developing country. (8 marks)

2 Describe factors that determine the rate of population growth. (4 marks)

3 Suggest reasons why population growth in developing countries is forecast to exceed population growth in developed countries. (4 marks)

4 Describe three ways developing countries can help less developed countries. (6 marks)

SUGGESTION FOR COURSEWORK

Investigate the size and role of local and national government in your country. What proportion of the total national expenditure (or Gross Domestic Product) is spent by the public sector? How does it finance its expenditure? What proportion of the total workforce is employed by the public sector? What goods and services does the public sector provide and why? In what other ways does government intervene in markets – for example, through price controls, laws and other regulations – which markets, and why? Consider the arguments for and against government intervention in markets.

Chapter 4

Production

The aim of production is to satisfy the wants of people. There are three main types of productive industries.

1 **Primary industries** include those firms who produce natural resources, for example – mining.
2 **Secondary industries** use raw materials to produce other goods. These industries are known as manufacturing industries.
3 **Tertiary industries** provide services.

Industries today are organized so that workers and firms specialize in the production of those goods and services at which they are best. High levels of output achieved by specialization are the result of this **division of labour** into separate tasks. One feature of production is the law of **diminishing returns**. This states that if one factor of production is fixed in supply, for example, land or capital, and extra units of another factor, for example, labour, are added to it, then the extra output or returns gained from the employment of each worker must after a time fall.

An entrepreneur's decision to produce will depend upon profits, profits being revenue received minus total costs. Total costs include variable costs, such as wages and raw materials, which depend upon the level of output, and fixed costs, like the rent of factory space. The **optimum level of output** of production or best level will be where the average cost of production is lowest.

When a firm increases its scale of production or employs more factors of production, average costs of production may fall. We say that the firm experiences **economies of scale** if it experiences cost savings from increasing the scale of production. Large-scale production can bring such benefits as the ability to buy in bulk, the use of specialized staff and machinery, low interest rate loans. However, if a firm grows too large, it may experience **diseconomies of scale**, or increases in cost, from increasing the scale of production.

Despite the advantages of large-scale production many firms remain small, preferring to offer personal service and to cater for local markets and individual needs.

MULTIPLE CHOICE

1 Which of the following would be regarded as secondary production?

   A Insurance
   B Coal-mining
   C Farming
   D Engineering
   E Entertaining

2 One advantage of the division of labour is:

   A Work becomes boring.
   B More goods and services are produced.
   C More training is needed.
   D People become too interdependent.
   E Products become standardized.

(continued)

3 In economics the short run refers to a period of time when:

A All factors of production can be changed.
B Land is fixed in supply.
C Capital is a variable factor.
D Labour is a variable factor.
E No more of any of the factors of production can be employed.

4 The following reasons can help explain why small firms can survive and flourish in the economy, *except*:

A Government schemes to aid small businesses.
B Local monopoly power.
C Small firms can change production techniques quickly.
D Lack of finance.
E Personalized service.

5 In the production of which of the following commodities are we likely to find the division of labour extensively applied?

A Portrait painting
B Disposable razors
C Made-to-measure suits
D Craft pottery
E Hairdressing

Questions 6–7 relate to the table of figures below which shows the total output of radios for different numbers of workers employed.

Number of workers employed	Number radios produced per week
1	100
2	210
3	325
4	425
5	500
6	540

6 The marginal product of the fifth worker employed is:

A 100
B 500
C 40
D 425
E 75

7 Diminishing returns to labour are experienced after the employment of worker number:

A 2
B 3
C 4
D 5
E 6

8 Which of the following are fixed costs?
1 Heating bills
2 Bank loan repayments
3 Wages
4 Electricity to run machines
5 Machine hire

A 5 only
B 3 and 5 only
C 1, 2 and 5
D 1, 2 and 4
E All of them

9 On the graph, what level of output represents the break-even point of production?

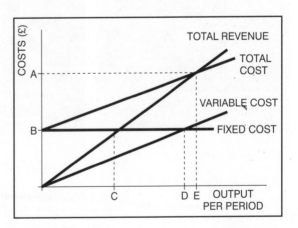

(continued)

Questions 10 to 13 relate to the following table of costs:

Total output of compact discs	Total costs
0	£100
100	£800
200	£1500
300	£2200
400	£2900
500	£3600
600	£4300

10 The average cost of producing 200 compact discs is:

A £7
B £70
C £7.50
D £1500
E £100

11 The fixed costs of production are:

A £1
B £10
C £100
D £800
E £1000

12 The variable cost of producing a compact disc is:

A £100
B £8
C £7
D £7.50
E £5

13 If the company produces 500 compact discs and wanted to make a £1400 profit from their sale, the price of each disc must be:

A £5
B £10
C £2.80
D £7.20
E £4.40

14 If a firm doubles all its factor inputs of land, labour and capital, and output more than doubles, we can say the firm has experienced:

A Constant returns to scale.
B Diminishing returns to labour.
C Economies of scale.
D Decreasing returns to scale.
E Increasing returns to scale.

DATA RESPONSE 1

A

B

C

1 The business organizations producing the goods and services in the photographs above have different motives for their productive activities. For each one suggest what their most important aim is likely to be.

(3 marks)

2 Which of the productive activities in the photographs is provided by industry in the **a** primary, **b** secondary, and **c** tertiary sector of the economy? (3 marks)

3 Provide another example of an industry in the **a** primary, **b** secondary, and **c** tertiary sector of the economy. (3 marks)

4 Over 75% of all employees in the UK are employed in the tertiary sector. Explain two reasons for this. (4 marks)

5 Photograph **B** shows an assembly line. Each worker in the assembly line performs a different task. Give two advantages and two disadvantages of this division of labour to **a** the firm, and **b** the employees. (8 marks)

6 The farm in photograph **A** wishes to expand production of crops from its existing land area by 30% over the next year. Suggest two possible advantages to the farm from increasing the scale of production. (4 marks)

DATA RESPONSE 2

Look at the photograph above of a large hotel in Tenerife. The costs of running the hotel are high.

1 Give an example of:
   a a fixed cost of running the hotel, (2 marks)
   b a variable cost of running the hotel.

2 Before the hotel was built, the land was used for farming. Explain which economic concept is involved in this change of land use. (2 marks)

3 The hotel is part of a large international chain. Discuss the possible advantages and disadvantages to **a** the owners of the hotel chain, and **b** the customers, of large-scale enterprise. (8 marks)

The table below shows the average production costs for crude oil from existing oil fields in a country.

Oil field	Average cost per barrel (US dollars)
A	$12
B	$19
C	$14
D	$20
E	$17
F	$23
G	$10

Over the last year the world price of oil has fallen from $25 per barrel to $18 as demand continues to fall and is outstripped by a glut of oil on the market. An oil industry spokesperson has said that unless oil prices rise two fields – responsible for around 20% of the annual oil production of the country – would be closed down.

The country was one of the world's largest oil producers, but over time production has fallen as older oil fields became exhausted. Exploration has identified several new oil fields with significant reserves, but they are offshore and very deep beneath the sea bed. Drilling these fields would require significant capital expenditures and average production costs are likely to be much higher than at existing oil fields. The government has recognised the need for the economy to diversify away from a dependence on oil through the development of other growth sectors.

1 What factors might explain the fall in demand for oil?   (4 marks)
2 Which oil fields still made a profit despite the recent fall in the world price of crude oil?   (2 marks)
3 If oil prices remain low, why do you think only two fields will close?   (4 marks)
4 What is capital expenditure? Explain using examples from the oil industry.   (2 marks)
5 What is meant by 'specialisation' and 'diversification'?   (4 marks)
6 Suggest why the country needs to diversify by developing other industries.   (2 marks)
7 Describe what might happen to the allocation of resources if the world price of oil increased and stabilised at $30 per barrel.   (4 marks)

A digital watch-making business faces the following costs:

Fixed costs   = £2000
Variable costs per watch   = £5

You are the accountant hired by the firm to work out the costs and revenues involved in producing watches in different amounts each month.

Watches produced per month	Total costs (£)	Average costs (£)	Total revenue (£)	Profit (£)
0			0	
500			3 500	
1000			7 000	
1500			10 500	
2000			14 000	
2500			17 500	
3000			21 000	
3500			24 500	
4000			28 000	

1 Calculate total costs in column two.   (9 × 1 mark)
2 Each watch is sold for £7.00 to shops, and the total revenue
   has been given in column four. Use this to calculate the profit
   or loss made at each level of output in column five.   (9 × 1 mark)
3 At what level of output will the business break even?   (2 marks)
4 In column three calculate the average cost of producing
   each watch.   (9 × 1 mark)
5 Explain what happens to the average cost of producing each
   watch as output rises, and why.   (4 marks)
6 What problems could the firm encounter if it tried to expand
   the scale of production beyond 4000 watches per month?   (4 marks)

SUGGESTION FOR COURSEWORK

Investigate productive activities in a local small business. How is production organised?

Identify different costs incurred running the business as fixed and variable costs. How do costs vary with the scale of production or level of service provided (for example, if a shop opened longer hours or a hairdresser's booked more appointments)?

At what level of output per period does the business break even at current prices and costs?

Suggest potential advantages and disadvantages to the business from expanding its current level of output or service.

Chapter 5

Types of Business Organization

It is the job of the entrepreneur to organize resources in a business or firm. In a modern economy there are many different types of business that an entrepreneur can choose from. Each type allows the entrepreneur to organize, manage, control the business and raise money in a different way.

Before starting up a business all entrepreneurs must ask themselves three questions:

1 *Will I have enough money?* Some businesses need more money than others. Small businesses that require little money are often **Sole Traders** or one person businesses. If more money is required a partnership may be formed. Large businesses are normally **Joint Stock Companies** or **Limited Companies**, many with thousands of owners all paying for a share of their company. Some of these firms may grow to become large **Multinationals** with operations located in different countries.

2 *Can I manage the business alone?* Sole traders have to be 'jacks of all trades' and do all the jobs necessary to run a business. **Partnerships** can employ people with a variety of skills, while the task of managing a **Joint Stock Company** can be left to a group of directors, chosen by the shareholders.

3 *Will I risk everything I own?* Some business owners have what is called **unlimited liability** whereby the owners stand to lose all of their possessions if they cannot afford to pay off business debts. However, some business owners may have **limited liability**. This means that if a business goes bankrupt the owners will only lose the amount of money they have put into the business.

Co-operatives are another form of business organization and are owned either by the shoppers who buy from them or by the workers who work in them.

Public sector organizations are owned or controlled by government. In the UK these are:

- the administrative offices of local government and central government.
- **Executive agencies** provide a number of public services, such as the provision of national statistics, passports and welfare benefits. These organizations are run in a business like way with independent control over how they spend the money allocated to them each year by central government.
- **Quangos** are quasi-autonomous non-government organizations. These are unelected government organizations runs by boards of directors to manage particular initiatives, for example regional health authorities, different research councils, and employment tribunals.
- **Public Corporations** are responsible for the day to day management of nationalised industries, owned by Central government. In the past, **nationalized industries** in the UK included coal mining, railways, and steel-making. There are very few nationalized industries left in the UK today following their sale to the private sector. This process is called **privatisation**.

1   Which of the following is not a private sector business organization?

   A   Public Limited Company
   B   Private Limited Company
   C   Partnership
   D   Public Corporation
   E   Consumer Co-operative

2   What is the minimum number of shareholders allowed in a Public Limited Company?

   A   20
   B   2
   C   7
   D   1
   E   9

3   If a business owner has limited liability, this means that:

   A   The business cannot go bankrupt.
   B   The owner must meet all debts.
   C   The business has sold shares.
   D   The business is only small.
   E   The owner cannot be asked to meet debts from his or her personal resources.

4   The maximum number of partners allowed in a partnership is:

   A   20
   B   2
   C   7
   D   50
   E   9

5   Which of the following is not a feature of the Private Limited Company?

   A   A minimum of two shareholders
   B   Shares can be sold on the Stock Exchange
   C   Shareholders have limited liability
   D   The company is managed by directors
   E   The company must hold an Annual General Meeting

6   Which of the following best describes a Public Limited Company?

   A   A company that has 29 partners
   B   A company owned by the Government
   C   A company that has factories and offices all over the world
   D   A company owned by its workers
   E   A company that is listed on a Stock Exchange

7   If the government privatises a state-owned industry by selling it to many different shareholders, the organization will become a:

   A   Partnership.
   B   Private limited company.
   C   Public limited company.
   D   Public corporation.
   E   Co-operative.

8   One of the main disadvantages of a large limited company is that:

   A   Shareholders have unlimited liability.
   B   Owners of the company can lose control to the directors.
   C   Specialization is not possible.
   D   There are no organized markets where shares in the company can be purchased.
   E   There is a lack of capital.

9   The best description of a Multinational company is:

   A   A company owned by governments in many different countries.
   B   A company that has its headquarters in one country but operates in many other countries.
   C   A company that is owned by shareholders all over the world.
   D   A company that enjoys large economies of scale.
   E   A company that has moved its plant from one country to another.

(continued)

10 The major difference between a Private Limited Company and a Public Limited Company is that:

A A Public Limited Company can sell shares on a stock exchange.

B A Public Limited Company is owned by its shareholders.

C A Private Limited Company is controlled by directors.

D A Private Limited Company must publish annual accounts.

E A Public Limited Company must hold an Annual General Meeting.

11 Which of the following is an advantage to a country of hosting a Multinational company?

A They may force other firms out of business.

B They may exploit cheap labour.

C They may switch profits between countries.

D They may have advanced technical knowledge.

E They may interfere in the politics of the country.

12 A furniture-maker produces to order expensive, hand-made pieces of wooden furniture. In which type of business organization is the furniture maker most likely to work?

A A public corporation

B A private limited company

C A retail co-operative

D A sole trader

E A public limited company

13 Which type of organization can issue shares on a stock exchange to raise capital?

A A sole trader

B A co-operative

C A private limited company

D A public corporation

E A public limited company

DATA RESPONSE 1

Buoyant EasyJet in £90 m cash call

Low-cost carrier EasyJet plans to raise £90 m by issuing new shares and to hire more staff.

The Luton-based airline, which floated on the market a year ago, is to issue 26 m new shares. As part of the deal, the company's chairman, Stelios Haji-Ioannou, will cash in 13 m shares worth nearly £50 m.

He will use the proceeds to finance other parts of his business empire, including the struggling internet cafe venture. As a result, his stake in EasyJet will be reduced from 32% to 25%.

The move has been made possible by buoyant figures from EasyJet showing an 82% increase in annual pretax profits to £40 m and a 1.5 m year-on-year improvement in passenger numbers,

Mr Haji-Ioannou said that the share issue would enable EasyJet to grow at a faster pace than planned: 'It is clear to us that a number of significant opportunities may now be arising in the form of new take-off slots at airports, planes and routes.'

Adapted from *The Guardian*, 31.10.2001

1 Suggest three reasons why businesses need capital. (6 marks)
2 How is EasyJet intending to raise capital? (2 marks)
3 What type of business organization is EasyJet? (2 marks)
4 The new owners in EasyJet will have limited liability. Explain what this means and why it will help EasyJet raise the new capital it needs. (4 marks)
5 Suggest two possible advantages to EasyJet from expanding the business. (4 marks)
6 Describe how ownership, control and finance of the EasyJet business organization will differ from a partnership. (6 marks)

DATA RESPONSE 2

The World's Biggest Multinational

GE is a diversified services, technology and manufacturing company with a commitment to achieving customer success and worldwide leadership in each of its businesses. It consists of 14 divisions which include aircraft engines, appliances, capital services, lighting, medical systems, plastics, power systems, electrical distribution and control.

GE operates in more than 100 countries and employs 313 000 people worldwide. In 2001 GE businesses owned assets worth $495 billion and generated a combined turnover of $126 billion.

The Company traces its beginnings to Thomas A. Edison, who established Edison Electric Light Company in 1878. In 1892, a merger of Edison General Electric Company and Thomson-Houston Electric Company created General Electric Company. GE is the only company listed in the Dow Jones Industrial Index today that was also included in the original index in 1896.

Adapted from *GE website, February 2002*

1 What is a multinational? (2 marks)
2 Explain three likely advantages to the GE business organization of its multinational structure (6 marks)
3 Explain the meaning of the statement 'GE businesses owned assets worth $495 billion'. (4 marks)
4 Suggest why GE may prefer to take-over an existing company in a country rather than starting up a new business in that country. (4 marks)
5 Most multinationals are public limited companies. How do these organizations raise finance to fund their multinational expansion? (2 marks)
6 Suggest three reasons why a government may encourage the location of GE businesses in its country. (6 marks)

PRIVATISATION IN ROMANIA:
More sales of assets are needed

The Government is rightly proud of the planned sale of Sidex, the steel mill that is the country's largest industrial plant and biggest single loss-maker. Barring accidents, Ispat International, the UK-based steel group, will complete the takeover of Sidex, complete with its 27 500 workers, at the end of the month.

However, bankers and lawyers involved in privatisation warn that although the Sidex sale, which involves promised investments of US$500 m, is important it does not by itself prove that the new social democrat government can implement privatisation any faster than its predecessors. As Ralph Hamers, country manager for ING, the Dutch financial group, says: 'Romania missed many opportunities when times were good. Now, the world is going into recession.'

Nevertheless, the new Government says it is putting more effort into making disposals. As well as Sidex it has sold Banca Agricola, the former farmers' bank, to Austria's RZB. The biggest item on the Government's sale list is a controlling stake in Banca Commerciale Romana, the largest bank, which is scheduled to be sold late next year, though the timing is tentative.

Other disposals under consideration include a slice of the Government's remaining shares in Romtelecom, the Romanian telecommunications utility, where OTE of Greece has 35 per cent and has indicated it would like to buy control. It already has management control through an agreement giving it management rights over 16 per cent of Government-owned stock. But any deal would be overshadowed by the general malaise in the industry.

The Government will be committed to selling 64 big companies under the terms of a US$300 m restructuring loan to be extended by the World Bank, once agreement is in place. These include big loss-making industrial plants such as the Roman truck company and Tractorul, the tractor maker.

Adapted from *The Financial Times, 3.10.2001*

1   What is privatisation?   (2 marks)
2   Suggest two economic arguments in support of privatisation.

                                                                      (6 marks)
3   Suggest two economic arguments against privatisation.   (6 marks)
4   How will the ownership, control and finance of a public limited company in the private sector differ from a state-owned organisation?   (4 marks)
5   A number of previously state-owned industries have been privatised into a number of smaller, competing companies. Examine the economic arguments for doing this.   (6 marks)
6   Some of the Romanian privatised companies have been or will be bought by foreign owned multinational companies. Do you think this will benefit the Romanian economy or not? Explain the reasons for your answer.   (6 marks)

1 Make a study of a small to medium-sized firm. It may be a manufacturing concern or a shop. The study should include a study of the ownership and control of the enterprise, how finance was raised, costs and revenues, and the problems that arise in running a business. The study should also include suggestions as to how the firm may be able to expand and the advantages and disadvantages of doing so.

2 Compare a government-owned organization with a public limited company in terms of:

   a ownership
   b control
   c finance
   d use of profits, if any.

Firms need money to start-up and to buy new capital equipment when they are ready to expand. Such money or capital may be classified either as **loan** or **risk capital**. Loan capital consists of money borrowed from a variety of sources such as banks, finance houses, wealthy individuals and governments.

Risk capital is raised by the sale of shares in the ownership of a company. Companies such as **pension funds**, **insurance companies**, **investment** or **units trusts** provide many millions of pounds to companies by buying their shares. Limited companies can raise money by issuing **debentures** or loan stock on a stock exchange. A debenture is simply and IOU issued in return for a loan of money.

In general there are two main types of shares which can be issued by a company to raise money. **Preference shares** promise to pay their owners a fixed dividend. **Ordinary shares** receive a dividend based upon what is left from profits after debenture holders and preference shareholders have been paid their share of the profit. Ordinary shares also carry voting rights at company annual general meetings.

People who buy stocks and shares are known as investors. Investors may buy these on the stock market. **Stock exchanges** run markets for the buying and selling of new and second hand stocks and shares.

There are two methods by which firms can grow in size. The first is by internal growth, where the firm increases its own size under its existing management or, more commonly, by **integration**, where one or more firms join together to form a larger enterprise.

A **takeover** occurs when one company buys all, or at least 50%, of the shareholding of another company, A **merger** occurs when two or more firms agree to form a new enterprise.

Horizontal integration occurs when firms engaged in the production of the same goods or services combine. **Vertical integration** occurs when two firms at different stages in a chain of production combine. **Lateral integration** occurs when firms producing different goods and services combine. This diversification is often called **conglomerate merger**.

MULTIPLE CHOICE

1 Which of the following statements is correct about the operation of a stock exchange?

   A It provides loan capital for businesses.
   B Market makers only act on behalf of the general public.
   C It trades in the shares of all limited liability companies.
   D It deals in second-hand stocks and shares.
   E It only deals with preference shares.

(continued)

Questions 2–5 consider these methods of raising finance:

A Preference shares
B Ordinary shares
C Debentures
D Gilt-edged securities
E Cumulative preference shares.

2 Which would be described as loan capital?

3 Which are issued by a government?

4 Which shares get their dividends first?

5 Which shares carry no voting rights?

Questions 6–8 consider the following people and firms who are connected with a stock exchange:

A Bears
B Bulls
C Market makers
D Stags
E Broker/dealers

6 Who buys up new share issues hoping their price will rise?

7 Who buys shares in the hope their price will rise?

8 Who has the function of providing a continuous market in stocks and shares, buying and selling shares on their own behalf?

Questions 9–12 consider the following forms of integration and growth for a firm:

A Horizontal integration
B Forward vertical integration
C Backward vertical integration
D Lateral integration
E Internal growth

Which of the above is most likely to give rise to each of the advantages below?

9 Control over their supply of raw materials.

10 Control over their retail outlets.

11 A wider range of products to reduce the risk of a fall in demand for one product.

12 Lower average production costs.

DATA RESPONSE 1

You are the manager of a commercial bank. You have been approached by a newly trained graphic designer seeking a bank loan for £10 000 over 5 years to start-up a new business. The business idea is for a printing shop in a busy high street. The shop will provide printing and photocopying facilities, personalized business cards, custom-designed wedding and other invitations, video and CD copying, individual T-shirt designs, and many other printed items for business and personal customers. There are two other similar shops already in the area – between 2 and 4 km away.

1 What factors will you take into account when deciding whether or not to loan the money to the new business venture? (6 marks)

2 The graphic designer is unaware that a sole trader will have unlimited liability for the business. Explain what this means. (4 marks)

3 Suggest alternative ways the small business could finance the following requirements:
   a premises
   b computer and copying equipment costing £3 000
   c regular orders for small stationary items
   d a company car.
   Explain the reasons for your choice of finance in each case. (8 marks)

4 Imagine now that it is two years later. The business has been a success and the owner now plans to open a further two print shops in other locations. Suggest two possible advantages and a potential disadvantage of this business expansion. (6 marks)

Publicis set to take over US rival

Publicis, the French advertising giant, is poised to announce a takeover of its US rival, Bcom3. A merger of the two groups would create the world's fourth-largest advertising group – Publicis and Bcom3 are currently ranked sixth and seventh respectively.

The deal is expected to be valued at more than £2bn and would allow the France-based group, which already owns Saatchi & Saatchi, to boost its presence in the US.

But negotiations are understood to have been complicated by Dentsu, the Japanese advertising group that has a 20% stake in Bcom3.

Dentsu will take a stake of between 10% and 15% in the merged company, according to a report in today's Wall Street Journal.

Adapted from The Guardian, 7.3.2002

1 What is a takeover? (1 mark)
2 How much is the takeover likely to cost Publicis? (1 mark)
3 Explain three ways (other than issuing new shares) that Publicis could finance the proposed takeover. (6 marks)
4 What type of business integration will occur from the takeover? (2 marks)
5 What is vertical integration? Suggest a business sector the advertising company could consider for forward vertical integration. (4 marks)
6 Explain the likely reasons why Publicis wants to takeover Bcom3. (8 marks)

DATA RESPONSE 3

Winchester turns film distributor

Winchester Entertainment, owner of Jellabies, the popular children's characters, is raising £22 m to allow it to branch into film distribution in Britain.

The first film it will handle will be a re-release of Raging Bull, starring Robert De Niro, at the end of this month. Up until now Winchester has only been involved in the sales side of film distribution in the UK.

The move will be financed by a share issue at 315p per share. Gary Smith, the chief executive, said: 'The funds will be used to develop the newly established UK film distribution business, to acquire rights to US studio-released films and to exploit the group's increasing catalogue of children's television rights.'

In addition, the money will be used for film development and marketing.

The company also announced a three-year deal with Wind Dancer, which produced the series Home Improvement and the film What Women Want, starring Mel Gibson and is expected to be released in the US in December.

Adapted from The Guardian, 3.11.2000

1 How does risk capital differ from loan capital to finance business expansion? (4 marks)
2 Which type of business organization is able to sell shares to the general public to raise capital? (2 marks)
3 How much capital is Winchester Entertainment hoping raise from the sale of shares? (2 marks)
4 Approximately how many shares will the company have to sell to raise this capital sum? (4 marks)
5 Describe the main differences between an ordinary share and a preference share. (6 marks)
6 Explain two financial reasons why investors may choose to buy shares in Winchester Entertainment. (4 marks)
7 Suggest three other ways Winchester Entertainment may have been able to raise capital. (6 marks)

SUGGESTIONS FOR COURSEWORK

1 Make a study of a local firm. How have they grown over time? Has it been a result of internal growth, merger or takeover? How have they raised the necessary finance for growth? Suggest how they may be able to grow in the future; for example, could they issue shares?
2 Make a study of how a stock exchange works. Why is it so important for industry and the economy?
3 Imagine you have savings amounting to £20 000. You decide to buy some second-hand shares. Using the share prices given in a daily newspaper, such as *The Financial Times*, or various share price websites, choose a range of shares on which to spend £20 000. Make a table of them, for example:

Week 1

Name of shares	Current price (pence)	Number bought	Amount spent (or total value)
B. Airways	120p	1000	£1200
Tesco	307p	800	£2456
...	...	...	...
...	...	...	...
...	...	...	...

Check the prices every week for a number of weeks and calculate the gain or loss you have made in the value of shares. Make suggestions why the prices of your shares have changed.

Chapter 7

The Location and Structure of Industry

Firms will locate their factories, offices, shops, etc. in places that yield the greatest advantages and involve the least costs. There are many factors that will affect their location decisions. Being near to their market or the source of their materials is clearly a very important consideration. However, if commodities are to be transported, suitable facilities like motorways or even airports may need to be close at hand. A supply of labour and low-cost land for large buildings are also necessary.

Exactly where a firm can locate its operations will often be a matter for local and/or national governments to decide. Firms will need to obtain planning consent to build new factories, offices or retail outlets. In many cases there may be a public inquiry so that local consumers, businesses, and residents can argue for or against a land use proposal.

Governments may also try to influence business location and expansion through a **regional policy**. For example, both the UK and European Union have operated a regional policy for many years to encourage firms to provide jobs and incomes in areas suffering from high levels of unemployment and industrial decline. In the UK these are called **assisted areas**. The UK Government offers grants to businesses moving to or expanding in these areas to help them pay for new premises and/or machinery.

Enterprise zones are smaller areas within UK cities that are in particular need of regeneration. The benefits available in an enterprise zone apply to both new and existing industrial and commercial business. These benefits may comprise generous allowances against tax for expenditures on industrial and commercial buildings, exemption from local business taxes, and a greatly simplified planning application process.

Many of the areas in need of regeneration in the UK, Europe and many other industrialised countries, are depressed because of **deindustrialization**. That is, primary and manufacturing industries, such as coal mining and steel making, have declined in these areas leaving many people without work and on low incomes. Most developed countries now employ far more people in service industries. For example, over 75% of employees in the UK work in service industries. In 1971 the proportion was just over 52%.

1 Which of the following manufactured products is likely to have undergone weight gain during production?

A Matches
B Cars
C Orange juice
D Processed meats
E Steel

2 Which of the following forms of government assistance are most likely to be offered to businesses as part of a Regional Policy to help depressed areas?

1 Grants for new capital expenditures
2 Simplified planning procedures
3 Paying the total wage bill of a business

A 1 and 2 only
B 2 and 3 only
C 2 only
D 3 only
E None of the above

3 Which of the following is a non-economic business location factor?

A The availability of government assistance.
B Proximity to key consumers.
C Proximity to golf courses for the business managers to use.
D A supply of skilled workers.
E Proximity to key suppliers.

4 A 'footloose industry' is one in which firms' location decisions are:

A Not affected by their market.
B Not affected by their source of raw materials.
C Not affected by transport links.
D Not affected by land values.
E Not affected by their market or source of raw materials.

5 If firms in one particular industry locate near each other they can benefit from:

1 A supply of skilled labour
2 Ancillary firms
3 Cheap land

A 1 only
B 1 and 2 only
C 2 and 3 only
D 3 only
E None of them

6 What is deindustrialization?

A An increase in the number of manufacturing firms in an economy
B A decrease in the number of manufacturing firms in an economy
C A growth in the importance of the service sector in an economy
D A decline in the importance of the manufacturing industry in an economy
E An increase in the number of jobs in the primary industry

Island forms bridge to the new economy

Mauritius Telecom's strikingly modern 21-storey tower in Port Louis may be the tallest building on the island, but according to Megh Pillay, the company's chief executive, it is already running out of space. 'Market growth has been so fast,' he explains.

Mauritius has just been connected to the new SAFE undersea fibre-optic cable, which by late 2001 will link the island to Malaysia, South Africa, and then onwards to West Africa and Europe. Just as importantly, France Telecom has just bought a 40 per cent stake in the company for US $261 m.

According to Mr Pillay, the venture will lead to a regional alliance – and as Mauritius nudges the limits of an island of 1.2m people (it already has a tele-density of 250 lines per thousand inhabitants), it will need to look towards the underdeveloped African market. It already has operations in Lesotho (with South Africa's Eskom and Zimbabwe's Econet), in Madagascar and in Mozambique. It is a sign of Mauritius' growing ambitions to become a telecommunications and IT hub.

From April to October, the mobile phone market has seen growth of 300 per cent. In November, Rogers Telecom — part of the island's largest holding company — launched Mauritius' first call centre, hoping to attract companies from Europe and elsewhere as they outsource their operations.

The Currimjee Group, which operates one of the island's two mobile phone companies, is moving in the same direction, and recently opened 'Trackmail', an internet-based call centre.

'I think there is a lot of opportunity because of our bilingual ability (French and English, as well as Hindi), our relatively competitive wage structure and educated workforce,' says Bashirali Currimjee, the chairman.

Deelchand Jeeha, the minister of information technology and telecommunications, is talking of a one-stop-shop cyber-city, software tie-ups with Indian companies, an internet gateway, and electronic governance. However, the finance ministry's recent review of the economy warns that 'although Mauritius has attained a high literacy rate, the quality of its labour force falls far short of what is needed for the country to move onto a higher plane of development'. Nearly 50 per cent of the labour force has only primary education, compared to 30 per cent in Singapore and 10 per cent in South Korea.

Until now, there has only been one internet service provider allowed on the island. Mauritius Telecom also enjoys a monopoly on fixed line Internet connections and is likely to do so until the end of 2003. And Emtel, the first mobile phone company on the island, has gone to the UK's privy council (still Mauritius' highest court) complaining about Mauritius Telecom's practices in the mobile sector. 'What has been lacking is a good regulatory authority,' says Mr Currimjee. 'For some time we feel there has been no real regulation of interconnections - we are having to pay what we feel is an extremely high price.'

Adapted from *The Financial Times, 18.12.2000*

You are the Chief Executive Officer of a multinational telecommunications company providing telephone and internet services. Your company is seeking new locations to expand its operations overseas. Read the article above and use the information it provides to help you answer the following questions.

1 What is a multinational company? (2 marks)

2 Explain the statement ' the mobile phone market has seen growth of 300 per cent'. (4 marks)

3 Explain the statement 'Mauritius Telecom also enjoys a monopoly on fixed line internet connections'. Why might this be a disadvantage for consumers? (4 marks)

4 Suggest three possible economic advantages to your company of locating a new telecommunications centre in Mauritius. (6 marks)

5 Suggest three possible economic disadvantages of a telecoms business location in Mauritius. (6 marks)

DATA RESPONSE 2

The following is an advertisement aimed at businesses to encourage their location in the East Durham Enterprise Zone in the UK.

East Durham Enterprise Zone is located at the heart of the thriving North East of England and is home to some of the regions major industrial estates. It is the ideal location for businesses with the major centres of Wearside, Tyneside and Teesside right on the doorstep and easy access to the rest of the UK and Europe. With Enterprise Zone status until December 2005 in a development area and with local financial benefits, no other site in the UK can offer your company an investment opportunity that makes better financial or operational sense.

There are main line stations at Durham and Newcastle with regular services to both London and Edinburgh. Airports at Newcastle and Teesside provide regular national and international flights. Five ports are also within an hours drive and make the area ideal for links to the major markets of the European Union.

Why it makes financial sense:

- 100% capital allowances on the construction of plants and premises
- 100% exemption from business rates
- Substantial grant aid towards capital investment
- Possible rent-free periods from developers
- A comprehensive range of financial incentives

Why it makes operational sense:

- Easy road access to Tyneside, Teesside and Wearside: the main business and consumer markets of this thriving region
- Easy access to the rest of the UK and Europe through excellent road, rail, air and sea links
- Proximity to major production centres in electronics, automotive industries, petrochemicals and engineering
- A highly skilled and flexible workforce
- A low cost of living in a quality region
- A streamlined planning process

1   The North East of England has suffered from deindustrialization. What is this? Suggest two economic measures you could use to quantify the scale of deindustrialization in an economy. (6 marks)

2   What is 'economic growth'? (2 marks)

3   Explain why the UK Government is keen to encourage economic growth in East Durham and other regional development areas in the UK. (6 marks)

4   Suggest four economic advantages to a business seeking a location in East Durham. (8 marks)

5   Discuss other ways a government could to try to encourage economic growth and higher levels of employment in an economy. (8 marks)

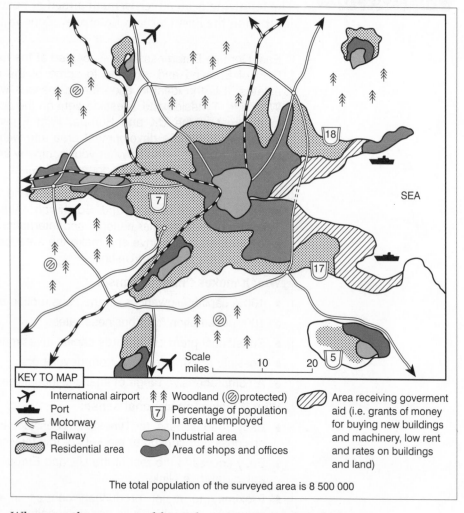

KEY TO MAP

- ✈ International airport
- ⚓ Port
- ≈ Motorway
- ∿ Railway
- ▨ Residential area
- 🌲🌲 Woodland (⊘ protected)
- ⑦ Percentage of population in area unemployed
- ▨ Industrial area
- ▨ Area of shops and offices
- ▨ Area receiving goverment aid (i.e. grants of money for buying new buildings and machinery, low rent and rates on buildings and land)

Scale miles — 10 — 20

SEA

The total population of the surveyed area is 8 500 000

Where on the map would you locate a new high-tech factory to produce computer memory chipsets? Discuss the reasons for your choice by comparing the economic advantages and disadvantages of your business location against other locations on the map.   (20 marks)

SUGGESTIONS FOR COURSEWORK

1   Arrange a visit to a local shop, office or factory and make a study of the factors you think influenced the owners's choice of location.

2   Are there any new motorways or major roads near you? How has this affected business location? Are there any new firms nearby? Make a study of the types of firms that have located near these roads. What are their similarities/differences?

3   Investigate the regional assistance policy of your national government. Which areas receive assistance and why? Evaluate the impact of the policy on a particular area is terms of regional GDP, employment, living standards and business location.

Chapter 8 | How Prices are Decided

The price of any commodity is determined by the forces of the demand for and supply of it. **Demand** is the willingness of consumers to buy goods and services at a number of given prices. In general as price rises the quantity demanded of a commodity contracts. **Supply** refers to the willingness of producers to make and sell a particular commodity. In general, as price rises quantity supplied rises.

A change in the price of a commodity will cause changes in the quantity demanded and supplied. The size of change will depend on their **price elasticity**. If a given change in price causes a more than proportionate change in quantity demanded and/or supplied then the demand and supply of that particular commodity are termed relatively **elastic**. If a given change in price causes a much smaller percentage change in quantity demanded and/or supplied they are termed relatively **inelastic**.

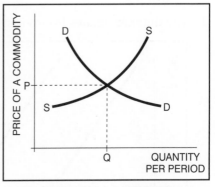

THE MARKET FOR A COMMODITY

Where the market demand for a product is equal to its market supply the **market price** of the product is determined. An increase in demand as a result of a rise in consumers' incomes, a change in tastes, a rise in the price of goods that could be **substitutes**, like butter and margarine, will force up the market price of the product. The **income elasticity of demand** measures the responsiveness of quantity demanded for a given product, given a change in the incomes of consumers. The **cross elasticity of demand** measures how much demand changes for a particular product, given a change in the price of a substitute or complement.

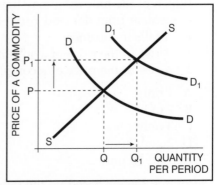

AN INCREASE IN DEMAND

An increase in the supply of a product resulting from technological progress, a fall in the cost of factors of production making it more profitable to produce the product, or perhaps just good weather in the case of farm produce, will tend to cause the market price to fall.

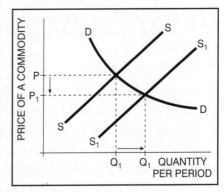

AN INCREASE IN SUPPLY

MULTIPLE CHOICE

1   A demand curve for a product is drawn on the assumption that all of the following remain unchanged *except*:

A   The price of the product.
B   Consumer tastes.
C   The price of other products.
D   The size of the population.
E   Incomes.

2   The diagram relates to product Z.

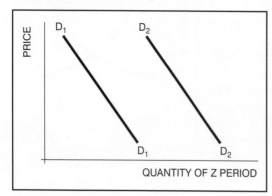

Which of the following may have caused a movement from demand curve D_1 to D_2?
1   A falls in incomes.
2   A rise in the price of a substitute.
3   A rise in the price of a complement.

A   1 only
B   2 only
C   3 only
D   2 and 3 only
E   1 and 2 only

Questions 3–6 are based on the following five terms. Which applies in each case?

A   Price elasticity of demand
B   Cross elasticity of demand
C   Income elasticity of demand
D   Price-elastic
E   Price-inelastic

3   After a fall in the price of a product total revenue from the sale of the good rises.

4   A measure of how responsive demand is to changes in people's incomes.

5   If the price of a substitute falls and the demand for another product rises we can measure this using what?

6   If the percentage change in the price of a good is less than the percentage change in the quantity demanded it causes, demand is said to be what?

Questions 7–8 are based on the following information. The income of a consumer rises from £100 to £120 while demand for the product falls by 40%.

7   What type of product is it?
A   Normal
B   Complementary
C   Substitute
D   Inferior
E   Price-elastic

8   What is the value of income elasticity of demand?
A   0.5   B   8   C   2   D   2.5   E   0.2

9   Demand for a product is likely to be price-inelastic:
A   The smaller the number of substitutes.
B   The smaller the number of complements.
C   The higher the price.
D   The greater the fraction of income spent on it.
E   The smaller the number of people who buy it.

10   The best explanation of the shift in the supply curve from SS to S_1S_1 would be:

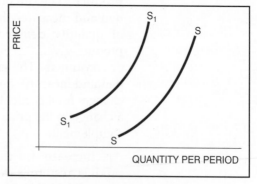

A   A rise in the price of the product.
B   The granting of a subsidy.
C   A fall in the price of raw materials.
D   Technical progress.
E   A rise in wages paid to labour.

(continued)

11 The cross elasticity of demand for a product is −5. The good is most likely to be:

A An inferior good
B A complement
C A substitute
D A normal good
E A free good

Questions 12–14 are based on the following diagram.

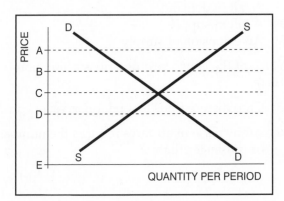

At which price will there be:

12 A market equilibrium?

13 The greatest excess demand?

14 The greatest excess supply?

15 If a bus company lowered its fare at peak times and total fare revenue fell, demand for bus travel at this time would be:

A Income-elastic
B Price-elastic
C Price-inelastic
D Income-inelastic
E Falling

16 If a rise in price from £1 to £1.10 caused supply to extend by 27%, price elasticity of supply would equal:

A 17
B 1.7
C 2.7
D 3.7
E 27

17 Which of the following pairs of commodities is an example of goods in complementary demand?

A Beef and lamb
B Coffee and tea
C Butter and margarine
D Quilts and quilt covers
E Salt and sugar

18 Other things unchanged, an increase in demand for a product will cause:

A Market price to rise and supply to contract.
B Market price to fall and supply to extend.
C An increase in supply as market price rises.
D An increase in market price and an extension of supply.
E Market price to rise with no change in quantity traded in the market.

Questions 19–21 are based on the following diagram.

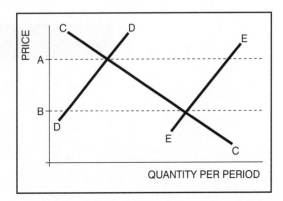

Given an increase in supply which curve or point indicates:

19 The increase in supply?

20 The new market price?

21 The demand curve?

(continued)

Questions 22–24 are based on the diagram below which represents changes in demand and supply in the market for chocolate bars.

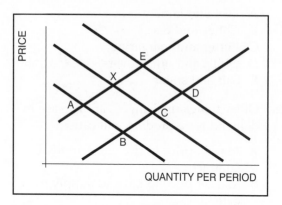

If X is the initial equilibrium where supply equals demand, find the new equilibrium positions given the following changes. (Take X as the original equilibrium in each case.)

22 A rise in people's incomes if chocolate is a normal good.

23 Technical progress in the chocolate-making industry.

24 A fall in the price of other sweets.

Questions 25 and 26 are based on the following terms:

A A contraction of supply
B A contraction of demand
C A fall in demand
D A fall in supply
E An extension of supply

Which of the above best describes a situation where:

25 Crop disease leads to a poor harvest of corn?

26 An increase in air fares reduces the number of passenger flights?

Below are the demand and supply schedules for a certain commodity.

Price (£)	Quantity demanded per month (000's)	Quantity supplied per month (000's)
10	10	40
9	15	35
8	20	30
7	25	25
6	30	20
5	35	14
4	40	8

1 Plot the demand and supply curves on a suitable graph and label them D and S respectively. (6 marks)

2 What is the market price and the quantity traded at this price? (2 marks)

3 Assume that the Government imposes a tax on the commodity of £1. Plot the new supply curve on your graph and label it S_1. (4 marks)

4 What is the new market price? (2 marks)

5 Imagine that the commodity in question is cigarettes. Why else may the supply of cigarettes fall? (6 marks)

6 If the demand for cigarettes is price-inelastic, what effect will the tax have on total spending on cigarettes? (2 marks)

THE HOTTER IT GETS THE MORE YOUR COCA-COLA MAY COST

Coca-Cola is testing a vending machine that automatically raises the price of the world's favourite soft drink when the temperature increases.

Adapted from *The Financial Times, 10.2.1999*

Opec announces oil output cut

The cartel that controls just under half of the world's oil production, Opec, agreed today to cut output by 1.5 m barrels a day, news that has pushed the price of a barrel of crude oil above $20 (£14).

Oil has tumbled on commodity markets due to lower demand after the September 11 attacks and a build-up of capacity among the world's major suppliers. Oil prices have fallen to as low as $16 (£11) a barrel from their peak of $35 (£24) per barrel in November last year.

Adapted from *The Guardian, 28.12.2001*

Read the articles above and, using your knowledge of demand and supply analysis, answer the following questions:

1 What is likely to happen to the demand for Coca-Cola soft drinks during hot summer months? (2 marks)
2 Explain why the change in demand for Coca-Cola will increase the price of the soft drinks. (2 Marks)
3 Illustrate the likely changes in the demand, price and quantity traded of Coca-Cola drinks during a summer month on a suitable diagram. (6 marks)
4 What is a cartel? (2 marks)
5 Explain why the OPEC decision to cut oil production is likely to increase the price at which crude oil is traded on the world market (2 marks)
6 What is meant by the price elasticity of demand for a good or service? (2 marks)
7 For which of the above products – soft drinks or oil – is demand likely to be more price elastic? Explain your answer. (4 marks)

Product group	Price elasticity of demand
Supermarket own label washing powder	−1.8
Bread	−0.5
Sausages	−2.4

A consumer research organisation has observed consumer spending patterns in a national supermarket chain to estimate the price elasticity of demand for the products above.

1 a What is price elasticity of demand?   (2 marks)
   b How is it calculated?   (2 marks)
2 If the price of each product group in the table increased by
   10% what will be the percentage change in market demand
   for each product group?   (6 marks)
3 For which product group above is demand price-inelastic?   (2 marks)
4 If demand for a product is price inelastic what will happen
   to revenues from the sale of that product if its price rises?   (2 marks)

The research organisation has also estimated a cross elasticity of demand of +0.5 for the leading brand washing powder with respect to changes in the price of the supermarket own-label washing powder.

5 a If the price of the supermarket brand was cut by 20% by
      how much will demand for the leading brand fall?   (2 marks)
   b Suggest why the cross-elasticity of demand for the leading
      brand is relatively inelastic.   (2 marks)
6 Explain how knowledge of the income elasticity of demand for
   different goods and services could help an entrepreneur decide
   on a new business venture.   (4 marks)

SUGGESTIONS FOR COURSEWORK

1 Undertake a survey of house prices.
   Using local newspapers and estate agents, find and compare properties for sale in different categories – for example, two-bedroom homes, three-bedroom homes, apartments, etc.
   Your survey should cover about three different areas near you. Work out the average price of each type of dwelling across all your areas.
   Describe the results of your findings and try to explain the differences in price between properties and areas. Your explanation should include discussion of the factors that influence the demand and supply of housing.

2 Investigate seasonal changes in the prices of different goods, for example, fruit and vegetables. Are winter prices of these goods higher than in summer? If this is so, try to explain why the prices of these commodities are likely to vary from season to season and within seasons using demand and supply analysis.

3 Undertake a survey of retail prices.

Select ten items of food or household goods bought on a regular basis by your family. Find out and note the price of each item in different types of shops, for example in a major supermarket and in small local retail outlets.

Explain why the prices of goods you have chosen vary between different retail outlets or shops.

Explain why small local shops continue to survive even though their prices may be higher than those in large supermarkets.

Chapter 9 | Social Costs and Benefits

When a firm produces a good or service it will only consider its own **private costs** and **benefits**. If the revenue from the sale of its commodity exceeds the costs of land, labour and capital involved in its production then it is profitable or commercially viable to use resources in this way to produce that commodity. However, the firm may not consider any costs it imposes on society. **External costs** may include harmful pollution of the atmosphere, noise and scenic pollution. Such external costs may be unacceptably high for society and they may be better off if the firm stopped producing its commodity. If, on the other hand, **external benefits** are high, society may want more than is currently provided. Indeed, it may be the case that because private production costs are so high, the commodity may not be produced at all for society to enjoy. For example, in many countries, loss-making passenger rail services are kept running by the government either by paying a subsidy to private sector train operators or by owning and operating these services in the public sector. The argument for doing this is based on the view that many people will be worse off without these rail services because they will have no alternative means of transport and there will be more road traffic congestion and pollution.

In general, if the **social costs** of production (private costs + external costs) exceed social benefits (private benefits + external benefits) society is better off if that particular commodity is not produced. Only if social benefits exceed social costs can the particular use to which resources are put be considered an **economic** use.

The same applies to consumption decisions. A person who smokes on a crowded bus may enjoy the private benefits of smoking but imposes external costs on others who would rather that person did not smoke.

Economists try to value external costs and benefits using **cost benefit analysis (CBA)**. Using CBA economists attempt to quantify external costs such as pollution, and external benefits in some common measure for comparison. Often this measure is money. However, this can be very difficult to do accurately.

1 An external cost is:

A A cost that a group of people pay for.
B A cost created by a firm which it pays for.
C A cost created by a group of people, or a firm, that others pay for.
D A cost created by society, that private firms pay for.
E A cost paid for by government.

2 In building an airport, the external costs might include:
1 The price paid for the land.
2 The loss of farming land.
3 The noise caused by construction.

A 1 and 2
B 1 and 3
C 2 and 3
D 1 only
E 2 only

3 Which of the following are external costs resulting from the consumption of cigarettes?
1 The cost of cigarette advertising.
2 The irritation caused to people who don't like smoking.
3 The medical care given to people who have smoke-related health problems.

A 1 and 2
B 2 and 3
C 1 only
D 3 only
E None of them

4 A particular use of resources is said to be economic if:

A Social costs = Private costs.
B Social benefits are greater than private benefits.
C Social costs are greater than social benefits.
D Private costs are less than private benefits.
E Social costs are less than social benefits.

5 If the production of a good or service results in high external benefits, but low private benefits, then:

A Private firms will produce more than society wants.
B Private firms will produce just enough to satisfy the wants of society.
C Private firms will produce less than society wants.
D Private firms will use resources to produce something else.
E The Government will produce the product.

6 Which of the following represents an external benefit?

A A firm that obtains a discount for buying materials in bulk
B A historic building blackened by traffic pollution
C An oil slick washed on to beaches
D An increase in a firm's revenue resulting from the success of its advertising
E A bigger supply of honey than usual for a bee-keeper thanks to his neighbour's garden flower display

Compost success fertilises botanic garden

There is one place in Britain where the Government's green tax is working as it should do – providing a huge increase in recycling along with investment in worthwhile environmental projects. That place is the Isle of Wight. Desperately short of land to create waste dumps, and needing to dispose of 138 000 tonnes a year of rubbish, the island's county council has been forced to take drastic action.

It has a £40 m deal under which 41% of domestic rubbish is being recycled – compared to an average 7.8% in the rest of Britain.

Island Waste, a subsidiary of Biffa, the waste company arm of Severn Trent Water, has re-equipped the council's dustcarts to separate kitchen waste, and is rebuilding an 'energy from waste' power station so it can be fuelled by waste pellets processed at a refuse collection plant next door, one that also removes and recycles aluminium cans.

The most striking investment is £2.2 m to build the UK's largest composting plant, a Canadian made machine that turns waste into compost within 14 days and can process 15 000 tonnes a year – more than can be used on the island at the moment.

The plant is responsible for a boom in organic farming. This year one of the island's biggest tomato growers intends to use the compost to grow his entire crop. The council also sells compost to gardeners and puts the rest on its parks and gardens.

This month the council closed one of its landfill sites, and within 15 to 20 years landfill will stop altogether. Any material that cannot be recycled will then have to be shipped to the mainland – making it very expensive.

Bruce Gilmore, general manager of Island Waste, is predicting that by next year more than 50% of rubbish will be recycled. 'We shall be expanding our doorstep collection, which already covers newspapers, to include three types of glass and possibly textiles,' he promised. The company is also trying to change attitudes to recycling by talking to schools and by targeting pensioners, the group most resistant to change.

Unlike some other schemes, distribution of landfill tax credits is given to a national body, the Royal Society for Nature Conservation, that has no connection with the waste industry. The main beneficiary on the Isle of Wight will be Ventnor botanic garden, which will get a visitors centre paid for by £600 000 from landfill tax and £830 000 from the Millennium Commission.

Another beneficiary will be the red squirrel, which will get new tree corridors.

The Guardian, 5.4.2001

1 Explain which economic concept is involved in a decision to use land for waste dumps instead of farming, housing or other uses. (2 marks)

2 In economics, what is the difference between a 'private cost' and a 'social cost'? (2 marks)

3 Explain the social costs of dumping waste in landfill sites. (4 marks)

4 From the article, what are the social benefits to the Isle of Wight of recycling waste? (8 marks)

5 Discuss the economic benefits to firms, such as farms, power stations and water supply companies, of changing their production and purchasing decisions to help reduce harm to the natural environment. (8 marks)

6 What policies might a government adopt to control external costs such as pollution? (4 marks)

Freeways swallow drivers' free time

Congestion on US highways is now so bad that the average American spends 36 hours a year sitting in traffic, a report published yesterday reveals.

Two years earlier, the average American spent 34 hours in traffic annually, compared with 11 hours per year in 1982, according to the Texas Transportation Institute at Texas A&M niversity, which studied congestion in 68 urban areas. The data was compiled by 11 state highway departments.

Congestion costs an estimated $78 bn (£55 bn) a year in wasted time and petrol, the institute said.

The most congested highways in the country were found in Los Angeles, California, where residents in 1999 averaged 56 hours a year – more than a working week's worth of time – in bumper-to-bumper traffic.

The study's co-author Tim Lomax, a research engineer, said that the building of transport infrastructure, including roads and bus and rail systems are not keeping pace with the construction of new housing and businesses across the country.

'It's a whole lot easier to start a manufacturing company or a software firm or build new housing than it is to put in a new highway or new street or even a new bus route,' he said.

A research group funded by the building industry warned that growing congestion on US highways could hurt the economy and jeopardise quality of life. 'Increasing traffic congestion nationwide threatens to put the brakes on the nation's economic growth,' William Wilkins, executive director of the Road Information Programme, said.

The Guardian, 8.5.2001

1 Explain why slow journey times caused by traffic congestion wastes resources. (2 marks)
2 How can traffic congestion increase business costs? (2 marks)
3 What is 'economic growth'? (2 marks)
4 Why are governments often involved in decisions about the building of major projects such as roads and railways? (4 marks)
5 Discuss why a failure to invest in new road and rail transport links may 'put the brakes on … economic growth'. (8 marks)

SUGGESTIONS FOR COURSEWORK

1 Is there a factory near you? Is there a motorway or main road near by? Do you live near an airport? Discuss the reasons for their location and how society appears to benefit or bears the cost of their location and use. A cost benefit analysis may be carried out to assess whether the use of resources is economic or not in your opinion.

2 Devise a campaign in your school or college to alert people to their own personal costs of smoking and to try to make them aware of the costs they may impose on society? Are there any benefits of smoking? For example, some people argue that smoking relaxes them and relieves tension and thereby enhances productivity at work. Cigarettes are also heavily taxed in many countries.

41

Chapter 10 | How Firms Behave and the Interests of Consumers

Firms are in competition to make as much profit as possible. Some firms try to increase profits by lowering their prices below those of competing firms. This is known as **price competition**. Firms can also raise their profits through **non-price competition** or by creating a want for their products through advertising, offering free gifts and easy credit.

How a firm behaves, the price it charges and the output it produces depend upon **market structure**. Market structure refers to the number of firms and amount of competition in an industry.

Perfect competition is a market structure where firms make perfect use of scarce resources. The use of resources is perfect because resources are always allocated efficiently to the production of the goods and services that consumers demand – that is, there is **consumer sovereignty**. The features of a perfectly competitive market are that all firms sell a homogeneous or identical product, no firm is able to influence the price it receives (that is, firms are price-takers) both producers and consumers have perfect information and firms are free to enter and leave an industry when they wish. Although perfect competition does not exist in reality, economists still need to know about it because the way in which our economy uses scarce resources may be improved by making markets more competitive.

The opposite to perfect competition is **monopoly**. A firm has a monopoly if it is the only supplier of a particular good or service. The main difference between monopoly and perfect competition is that monopolies can charge higher prices and produce a lower output than under perfect competition. Because of the lack of competition monopolies may also provide a poor service and can influence consumer wants.

Monopolists are able to do this because they are price-makers, that is, they can fix their own price. They tend to engage in non-price competition such as advertising, they can make abnormally high profits and they may use **barriers to entry** to keep other firms out of the industry. These barriers to entry may be **natural**, for example, a firm may own the only supply of a particular resource, or **artificial**, for example, a monopoly may try to stop its suppliers from supplying any new competitors.

Monopolies, because they produce such a large output, can often experience economies of scale and so can sometimes charge a lower price than under competition. Monopolists also make large profits and can use these to pay for research and development into new products.

A small group of large firms may work together to become a type of monopoly by keeping prices high. Firms acting in this way are called a **cartel**. When there are only a few firms in an industry these firms are called **oligopolies**.

Many goods and services are produced under **monopolistic competition**. This market shares features of both competition and monopoly; its main feature is **product differentiation**. Product differentiation happens when each firm sells its own brand of good – for example, different brands of soap. Each firm has a monopoly in the brand it produces, but also faces competition from other similar brands. This type of firm often uses advertising to create a **brand image**. Such advertising may be **informative** or **persuasive**.

The consumer is legally protected from the restrictive and unethical practices of some enterprises in many countries. For example, in the UK **consumer protection laws** cover all aspects of commerce including trade descriptions, weights and measures, food hygiene, and consumer credit. **Competition policy** regulates the behaviour of firms to make sure they compete and operate fairly. Firms found guilty of abusing their market power can be fined heavily, and in some significant cases may be forced to break up into smaller competing enterprises.

MULTIPLE CHOICE

1 Which of the following is not a feature of perfect competition?

A Homogeneous product
B Perfect information
C All firms are price-takers
D There are barriers to entry
E Consumers can buy from a large number of firms

2 Which of the following would help a monopoly to prevent competition?
1 It benefits from economies of scale.
2 It uses a patent to protect its product.
3 Its average costs are higher than a smaller firm's.

A 1 only
B 2 only
C 3 only
D 1 and 2
E 1 and 3

3 Which of the following could be an advantage for consumers under a monopoly?

A It charges high prices.
B It has a motive to research and develop new products.
C It prevents new competing firms from entering the market.
D It restricts output.
E Producer sovereignty.

4 Which type of government policy will involve control of monopolies?

A Monetary policy
B Fiscal policy
C Trade policy
D Competition policy
E Social policy

5 Which of the following are arguments for privatization?
1 It raises revenue for the Government.
2 It breaks up economies of scale.
3 More competition lowers prices.

A 1 only
B 2 only
C 3 only
D 1 and 2
E 1 and 3

6 Monopolistic competition differs from perfect competition in which of the following ways?

A There are a large number of competing firms.
B Products are differentiated.
C Firms are free to enter the market.
D Market prices are determined by the forces of demand and supply.
E There are a large number of consumers.

(continued)

43

7 Which of the following is most likely to be the subject of persuasive advertising?

   A A bus timetable
   B A doctors surgery
   C A fizzy drink
   D A restaurant menu
   E Employment regulations

8 If the dominant firm in a market restricts the supply of the product it sells, the most likely outcome is:

   A A fall in demand for that product.
   B A price war with rival suppliers.
   C A fall in product quality.
   D A fall in the profits of the firm.
   E A rise in the market price of the product.

DATA RESPONSE 1

UK Government will tackle big banks

The UK Government is thought to be preparing to increase competition in a sector dominated by four players by telling retail banks that they must make it easier for small businesses to move their accounts.

Endorsing the recommendations of the Competition Commission report into small business banking, the Government may also ask the biggest banks to 'share' their branches with rivals which do not have extensive networks. This would enable smaller banks to offer accounts for small businesses.

During its investigation, the Competition Commission told the banks that a 'complex' monopoly existed in the provision of banking services to small businesses and that Royal Bank of Scotland had a 'scale' monopoly as a result of its takeover of NatWest. This means that the 'big four' – Royal Bank of Scotland/NatWest, HSBC, Barclays and Lloyds TSB – provide banking services to 90% of small business. Those banks argue that this is the result of their large networks which are considered important for small businesses because they need easy access to branches, to pay in cash, for instance.

The report from the commission had been delayed from last summer because of dispute with the banks over how to calculate whether the sector was making excess profits from business customers. The UK government said the delay had been necessary to 'enable the Competition Commission to consider further arguments and evidence from the banks'.

Adapted from *The Guardian*, 13.6.2001 and 7.1.2002

1 What is the role of the Competition Commission in the UK? (4 marks)

2 What evidence is there in the article to suggest the main UK commercial banks jointly operate a monopoly? (6 marks)

3 What further evidence would you need to decide whether the UK banks were making 'excess profits' from their monopoly? (6 marks)

4 The article suggests the Competition Commission may require the big UK banks to share their branches with smaller rival banks with fewer branches of their own.

   a How might this benefit bank customers? (4 marks)

   b What other measures could the Commission recommend to reduce any 'excess profits' from the banking monopoly? (4 marks)

5 Suggest two examples of non-price competition that may take place between the main UK commercial banks. (4 marks)

6 Explain the difference between informative and persuasive advertising using possible examples the banking sector might use. (6 marks)

Government intervenes in battle for P&O Princess

The Government yesterday stepped into the increasingly bitter battle for control of P&O Princess Cruises by referring a proposed £4.2bn merger with Royal Caribbean to the Competition Commission.

The two cruise lines said they remained confident of success although the commission could call for them to sell off some of their businesses. This may make it harder to ward off Carnival, the US rival that has made a hostile takeover bid of £3.5bn bid for Princess.

Carnival – anxious to keep its ranking as the world's biggest cruise company – said the referral of the proposed merger to the Competition Commission made it "indefensible" for P&O Princess' management not to open takeover talks with them

Patricia Hewitt, the UK trade and industry secretary, said: "The Director General of Fair Trading has advised me that there remain sufficient competition concerns surrounding this merger to warrant a reference to the Competition Commission." The outcome of the review, due on May 20, should not be prejudged.

P&O Princess shares remained steady at 399p yesterday and chief executive Peter Ratcliffe shrugged off the setback. "Notwithstanding this reference, we are confident that we will receive clearance once the Competition Commission has fully reviewed the substantive facts and issues surrounding our combination with Royal Caribbean."

Adapted from *The Guardian*, 30.1.2002

1 What is a merger? (2 marks)
2 Which two companies in the article plan to merge? (2 marks)
3 What are the likely advantages of merger to these companies? (4 marks)
4 How might consumers benefit from the merger of the two companies into a larger enterprise? (4 marks)
5 A rival company has made a 'hostile takeover' bid for one of the companies planning to merge. Explain what this means and how it differs from a merger. (4 marks)
6 Suggest why the UK Government has 'competition concerns' with the proposed merger. (4 marks)
7 If you were asked to investigate whether the proposed merger would reduce competition, what information would you need to know? (8 marks)
8 Suggest the ways in which the merged company could create a new brand name and image for its services. (6 marks)

SUGGESTIONS FOR COURSEWORK

1 The petrol market is a good example of a market where a handful of large firms dominate the supply of the product – for example, Shell, Esso, BP, Amoco.

   Petrol prices are often changing, but are petrol companies competing on price? What other methods of competition do they use? Collect information on prices and other forms of competition among these petrol companies. Is there evidence of restrictive practices among these firms to try to keep out new smaller competing petrol station companies? Write a report of your findings and thoughts.

2 Devise a detailed advertising campaign for a particular product, for example, a washing powder or perhaps a computer game. Who should the product be aimed at? What brand image will you create? Give reasons for when and where you will advertise. Collect information on how much advertisements will cost from writing to newspapers and magazines or even television companies.

3 Identify a recent investigation by a competition authority. What was the investigation about? What competition concerns were raised? What information did the authority consider, and what was its findings? Did the competition authority recommend any actions be taken, and why?

Chapter 11   The Labour Market

To produce goods and services firms must buy or hire factors of production. The price of **labour** is the wage rate and like the price of any other commodity it is determined by the forces of demand and supply. The forces are such that as wages rise so the demand for labour contracts but the supply expands as more workers are willing to work.

Any increase in the demand for labour will cause wages to rise. Because the demand for labour is a **derived demand** – that is, derived from consumers' wants for goods and services – then any increase in consumers' demands will increase the demand for labour. Any increase in labour productivity will also cause firms to demand more labour.

An increase in **productivity** means that more output or revenue can be produced from the same input of labour and other resources. A firm may improve its competitiveness and profitability by increasing productivity through revised working practices, the research and development of new products and processes, replacing old equipment and machinery, and encouraging workers to greater levels of effort through training and performance related pay and other bonus schemes.

The **working population** in a country consists of all people willing and able to work; it forms, therefore, the total supply of labour in that country. However, the supply of labour to a particular occupation will depend on many factors ranging from how much the job pays to the level of job satisfaction and promotion prospects. All the things that affect the attractiveness of a job are called its **net advantages**. Changes in the attractiveness or net advantages of jobs will cause changes in the supply of labour to those jobs. A rise in the supply of labour to an occupation will depress its wages, while if labour is in short supply wages will rise to try and attract more workers. How easily workers can change their jobs is known as **labour mobility**.

Wage differentials between different groups of workers in different occupations, industries and/or regions can be explained by differences in labour market demand and supply conditions. For example, workers with skills in short supply relative to employers' demand for their skills will tend to attract high wage rates.

A **trade union** is an organised group of workers who have joined together with the purpose of improving wages and working conditions. Trade union membership and the number of unions in the UK have declined over time. Many unions are affiliated to the **Trade Union Congress (TUC)**.

To regulate relations between trade unions and their employers there are employer associations in the UK such as the National Farmers Union and the National Federation of Building Trades Employers. Many of these associations are affiliated to the **Confederation of British Industry (CBI)**.

Unions may try to raise their members' wages at a faster rate than productivity gains by reducing the supply of labour to an occupation or industry. A **single union agreement** between a trade union and an employer or group of employers means that one union will represent all the workers in a firm or industry. A union may also restrict membership to only those workers who have served long apprenticeships and skills training. In some cases a union may restrict the supply of labour from its membership to almost nothing through strike action in an industrial dispute with an employer or group of employers.

Discussions between employers and unions are known as **collective bargaining**. While most disputes are settled in this way, sometimes unions and employers cannot agree. When this happens an organization, set up by the UK Government, known as ACAS (the **Advisory, Conciliation and Arbitration Service**), can help both sides reach an agreement.

The **government** is a major employer in many countries but may also intervene in labour markets: to influence the level of employment in the economy; to restrict the bargaining power of some trade unions; to protect the rights of employees and employers through employment and health and safety laws; and to set minimum wages for low-paid workers.

MULTIPLE CHOICE

1   The following table relates to productivity in a firm.

Unit of labour	Value of output per week £
1	300
2	320
3	290
4	230
5	150

If the weekly wage rate is £290 the firm will employ which of the following number of labour units?

A   1
B   2
C   3
D   4
E   5

2   The demand for labour is said to be a derived demand because:

A   It depends on firms' profits.
B   It depends on the scarcity of other resources.
C   It depends on its wages.
D   It depends on the demand for goods and services.
E   It depends on the price of complementary goods.

3   If a firm employs 200 workers who produce 1000 units of a good each day, labour productivity per day is:

A   2 units.
B   1000 units.
C   200 units.
D   5 units.
E   50 units.

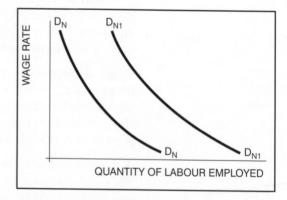

4   The best explanation for the rise in demand for labour from D_N to D_{N1} is:

A   A fall in wages.
B   A fall in the price of the product they produce.
C   An increase in unemployment.
D   Technical progress.
E   Increasing productivity of labour.

5 The working population in the United Kingdom includes all of the following except:

A Students.
B The unemployed.
C The self-employed.
D The armed forces.
E Employees.

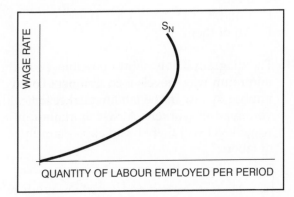

6 The supply curve shows that:

A Wages fall as the amount of labour increases.
B A rise in wages reduces the size of the working population.
C After a certain level of wages labour chooses more leisure than work.
D Supply rises as wages rise.
E Wages have no effect on the supply of labour.

7 The supply of labour to an occupation will tend to rise:

1 The better the promotion prospects.
2 The fewer perks there are.
3 The greater the amount of job satisfaction.

A 1 only
B 2 only
C 3 only
D 1 and 3
E All of them

8 The wages of carpenters will tend to rise if:

1 The supply of carpenters falls.
2 Their productivity rises.
3 The price of wooden products falls.

A 1 only
B 2 only
C 3 only
D 1 and 2
E All of them

9 Re-training the unemployed can have which of the following advantages?

1 Increase their occupational mobility
2 Increase their geographical mobility
3 Increase their chances of work

A 1 only
B 2 only
C 3 only
D 1 and 2
E 1 and 3

10 Which of the following reasons may account for differences in wages between two jobs?

1 Unsociable hours of work
2 Regional differences in the cost of living
3 Different qualifications are required

A 1 only
B 2 only
C 3 only
D 1 and 2
E All of them

11 A single union agreement may have which of the following advantages for an employer?

1 It reduces time spent negotiating with unions.
2 It increases the union's bargaining power.
3 It protects the skill of workers in the union.

A 1 only
B 2 only
C 3 only
D 1 and 2
E 1 and 3

12 A union takes strike action over a claim for wages. Which of the following factors will give them more power?

1   A closed shop
2   If they produce essential services like electricity
3   If wages are only a small percentage of total costs

A   1 only
B   2 only
C   3 only
D   1 and 2
E   All of them

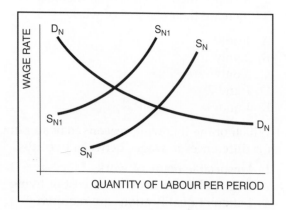

QUANTITY OF LABOUR PER PERIOD

13 What has happened in the diagram to the equilibrium wage and employment?

A   Wages and employment have risen.
B   Wages and employment have fallen.
C   Wages have risen; employment has fallen.
D   Wages have fallen; employment has risen.
E   No change in either.

14 Women often tend to earn less than men because:

1   The often work part time.
2   Employers don't like the possibility of them going on maternity leave.
3   Married women appear less mobile than men because of family ties.

A   1 only
B   2 only
C   3 only
D   1 and 2
E   All of them

15 Which of the following initiatives can help raise productivity in a firm?

1   Training workers in new and improved skills
2   Performance related pay schemes
3   New production methods and working arrangements

A   1 only
B   2 only
C   3 only
D   1 and 3
E   All of them

16 The diagram below shows possible minimum wage levels a government could impose by law in the labour market for young adult workers. At which minimum wage level will there be an excess supply of labour?

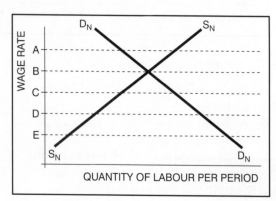

QUANTITY OF LABOUR PER PERIOD

Male and Female Average Weekly Pay (including overtime) Selected occupations UK April 2000

Occupation	Male £	Female £
Bus and Coach Drivers	287.3	245.5
Librarians	428.8	395.8
Nurses	431.5	407.0
Solicitors	801.6	682.3
Waiters/Waitresses	189.2	178.6

Source: *ONS 'New Earnings Survey' 2000*

1 What do you notice about the female and male earnings given in the table above? (2 marks)

2 Explain why you think differences in earnings between males and females occur. (4 marks)

3 Carefully explain why you think the average weekly pay of solicitors is higher than the other occupations listed? (4 marks)

4 a Give two reasons why there might be an increase in the demand for nurses. (4 marks)

   b Give two reasons why the supply of nurses may fall. (4 marks)

5 Suggest two factors which could explain the increase in female employment observed over time in many countries. (4 marks)

6 Give two reasons why the gap between male and female earnings has been closing. (4 marks)

Number of trade unions and union members; Great Britain 1975–1999

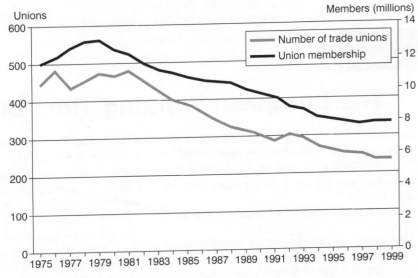

Labour Market Trends, September 2001

1 How has trade union membership in Britain changed over time? (2 marks)
2 What key factor can help explain this change? (2 marks)
3 What is a single union agreement? (2 marks)
4 Suggest one advantage to workers and one advantage to a firm from a single union agreement. (4 marks)
5 What is collective bargaining? (2 marks)
6 Suggest two reasons a trade union may take industrial action against an employer or group of employers. (2 marks)
7 Describe the role ACAS may play in an industrial dispute. (4 marks)

Percentage annual change in labour productivity (real output per person employed)

	1997	1998	1999	2000
UK	1.7	1.1	0.4	2.0
France	1.9	2.1	1.3	1.5
Germany	2.3	1.8	1.1	2.3
USA	2.1	2.1	2.1	1.1
Japan	0.3	−2.2	2.1	1.1

Adapted from *European Economy, 1999 review*

1 What is 'productivity'? (1 marks)
2 Using the table in which economy did productivity **a** increase the most and **b** the least over the period 1997–2000? (2 marks)
3 Suggest factors that may explain the differences in productivity growth observed in the different economies in the table. (4 marks)
4 How might an increase in productivity affect **a** the costs and **b** the profits of firms? (2 marks)
5 Describe three ways a firm can attempt to increase the productivity of its resources. (6 marks)
6 Explain how raising productivity can improve the standard of living in an economy. (2 marks)

The European Working Time Directive

The European Working Time Directive became law in the UK in 1998. The directive established a number of minimum employee rights including;

- an average working week of not more than 48 hours
- a minimum rest period of 11 hours in every 24 hours
- uninterrupted rest periods of 24 hours in each seven-day period
- a minimum of 4 weeks annual paid holiday

- free health assessments and insurance for nightworkers

Trade unions welcomed the new legislation as helping to reduce accidents and sickness in the workplace, and improving working conditions for millions of employees.

The UK had resisted the European Union directive since 1993. Employers have argued it will impose 'crippling costs' on businesses and could reduce employment.

1 What is the 'European Union'? (2 marks)
2 What is a 'trade union'? (1 mark)
3 Suggest how the European Working Time Directive could increase business costs and reduce employment. (4 marks)
4 What are the economic advantages of training to **a** employees, **b** firms, **c** an economy? (6 marks)
5 Describe the costs to an economy of a high level of unemployment. (6 marks)
6 Discuss supply side policies a government might use to increase employment in an economy. (8 marks)

Look at this table showing how much labour is demanded and supplied at given wage rates in the aero-engine manufacturing industry.

Wage rate per hour	Quantity of labour demanded	Quantity of labour supplied
£10	100	50
£20	70	70
£30	40	90
£40	10	110

1 Plot on a suitable graph the labour demand and supply curves and label them. (4 marks)
2 What will be the equilibrium wage rate and how many workers will be employed in aero-engine manufacture? (4 marks)
3 Suggest how each of the following may affect the equilibrium wage and level of employment in the firm:
   a An increase in labour productivity
   b A fall in the supply of engineers
   c A fall in the demand for aircraft
   d An increase in the pay of engineers in other manufacturing industries
   e A fall in the price of capital equipment
   Explain your answers, using diagrams where possible. (8 marks)

SUGGESTIONS FOR COURSEWORK

1 Choose a mixture of different jobs in both manufacturing and services. For each of the jobs you have chosen, find out about the levels of education and skills needed to do the job. Compare these requirements to the wage paid.
   Investigate whether or not the jobs requiring more skills and education pay more. If not, comment on the factors which might explain this.

2 Find out about a recent dispute between an employer and a union. Investigate **a** the causes of the dispute, **b** what both sides did during the dispute and why, **c** the result of the dispute.

Analyse the effects of the dispute and the settlement on:

a union members   **b** employers   **c** consumers   **d** the economy.

3 Investigate government and private sector schemes for training labour. Find out the aims of these schemes and report on their effect on labour supply, employers and the health of the economy. (You could interview people on government training schemes as well as the people leading the schemes.)

4 Find out about the changing structure of employment – for example, the increase in female and part-time workers. Investigate the reasons for change and analyse how it is likely to affect unemployment, consumers, producers and the economy.

Chapter 12

How the Economy Works

The total amount of output produced in an economy each year is known as the **national output** while the total amount of income earned in an economy is its **national income**.

If we assume a simple economy has no government or foreign trade then the only two decision-makers are private households and firms. Households will trade their factors of production in return for incomes from firms. In turn they will spend their incomes on firms' goods and services. If all income is spent on this **consumption** then it should be clear that national income, expenditure and the value of output will all be equal. Indeed, this still holds when a government and foreign trade are included.

Not all income will be spent on domestic goods and services. Some part of households' income may be saved, paid in tax or spent on imports. Any increase in these **leakages** from the flow of income and expenditure in the economy will reduce demand for domestic output and result in rising unemployment and falling national income.

On the other hand, firms may invest money in new capital, a government may spend money on the provision of goods and services and foreign countries may buy exports. Any increase in these **injections** of income into the economy will boost demand and raise employment and national income.

Changes in total or **aggregate demand**, resulting from changes in consumption expenditure, investment, government spending or export expenditure, can have widespread effects on the economy. The **multipler** explains how an initial change in aggregate demand may have a much larger effect on output, employment and national income. For example, if there is a fall in demand for UK cars the production of cars will be cut and car workers will find themselves out of work. They now have less income to spend on goods and services. Shops suffer and reduce their orders of goods and services from wholesalers and manufacturers. The fall in demand is now general and causes many more firms to cut production and shed jobs. Employment, output and national income continue to fall.

When economists try to calculate the value of National Output or National Income they must remember that some part of the total output in an economy may be made up of imported materials and their value must be deducted. This will give a figure for the total value of output produced by all domestic firms in the economy. This is known as the **Gross Domestic Product (GDP)**. However, this does not give us the final total of commodities available to people in the economy as some income is earned from firms and property owned abroad, and from shareholdings and loans made abroad. These incomes must be added to calculations of GDP. Similarly, any incomes earned in the economy by people abroad must be deducted. The difference between the flows of income entering and leaving an economy is known as **Net Property Income from Abroad**. When we add this figure to GDP we obtain the **Gross National Product (GNP)**.

Net National Product (NNP) or national income is GNP minus **depreciation**. Over time the value of the stock of capital in the economy falls as a result of wear and tear. This depreciation has to be deducted from GNP to get a true value of what the country has produced over and above the output needed simply to replace old and worn-out capital.

MULTIPLE CHOICE

1 Aggregate demand consists of, among others:
   1 Public expenditure.
   2 Expenditure on imports.
   3 Savings.

   A 1 only
   B 2 only
   C 3 only
   D 1 and 2
   E All of them

2 Which of the following is a leakage from the circular flow of income of an economy?

   A Spending on exports
   B Spending on imports
   C The interest on a savings account
   D Welfare payments
   E Student loans

3 The largest component of aggregate expenditure in most countries is:

   A Public expenditure.
   B Investment in capital goods.
   C Expenditure on exports.
   D Investment in stocks of consumer goods.
   E Consumption expenditure.

4 All of the following normally occur in a boom except:

   A Rising national income.
   B Rising output.
   C Rising unemployment.
   D Rising prices.
   E Rising demand.

5 Which of the following may cause a rise in consumption expenditure?

   A A rise in interest rates
   B A rise in income taxes
   C A rise in welfare payments
   D A rise in unemployment
   E A fall in the population

6 A fall in investment may cause:
   1 A fall in output.
   2 A fall in employment.
   3 A fall in national income by a far greater amount than the fall in investment.

   A 1 only
   B 2 only
   C 3 only
   D 1 and 2
   E All of them

7 UK property income from abroad will include all of the following, except:

   A Profits from UK factories in Germany.
   B Dividends on shares in Spanish companies held in the UK.
   C Interest on loans to the UK.
   D Rent from land owned in America by UK residents.
   E Interest on UK loans made to France.

8 Net National Product or national income is equal to:

   A Gross Domestic Product minus National Product.
   B Gross National Product minus Gross Domestic Product.
   C Gross Domestic Product plus indirect taxes minus subsidies.
   D Gross National Product minus depreciation.
   E Depreciation minus Gross National Product.

(continued)

9 If there is inflation in an economy because of too much demand for a limited amount of goods and services, it may be reduced by a rise in which of the following:

1 Savings
2 Imports
3 Investment

A 1 only
B 2 only
C 3 only
D 1 and 2
E All of them

10 If unemployment is caused by a low level of aggregate demand it may be reduced by:

1 A rise in spending on imports.
2 A fall in consumption expenditure.
3 A rise in public expenditure.

A 1 only
B 2 only
C 3 only
D 1 and 2
E All of them

Questions 11 and 12 relate to the following figures:

	£ million
Gross Domestic Product	89
Property income from abroad	18
Property income paid abroad	15
Depreciation	6

A £72 million
B £89 million
C £86 million
D £82 million
E £92 million

11 What is the Gross National Product?

12 What is the Net National Product or National Income?

DATA RESPONSE 1

Industrial output plummets

Manufacturers are sacking workers at the fastest pace since the last recession as firms struggle to ride out the first synchronised downturn in the world economy for more than 20 years, the latest snapshot of the UK sector showed yesterday.

Industry ended 2001 on a low note, with output falling in December for the 10th month in a row, according to the Chartered Institute of Purchasing and Supply. The pace of decline is accelerating, and analysts warned that the survey suggested there was worse to come. "This confirms that a recovery in industry is not even on the radar screen," said Daniel Kaye at Capital Economics. "Whatever happens to consumer spending, it looks almost certain that policymakers will be operating amidst an environment of deep manufacturing recession".

The nature of the twin-speed economy was highlighted by separate data yesterday that pointed to continued strength in both commercial and residential property and improving conditions in the services sector.

Adapted from *The Guardian* and *The Daily Telegraph*, 3.1.2002

1 What is 'manufacturing'? (2 marks)
2 What is meant by a 'recession'? (2 marks)
3 Describe two economic characteristics associated with recession. (4 marks)
4 Suggest two disadvantages to workers in a region specialising in manufacturing industry. (4 marks)
5 If consumer spending declines which other sector of the UK economy is most likely to be affected? (2 marks)
6 Discuss how the government could use fiscal and monetary policies to help the economy recover from recession. (8 marks)

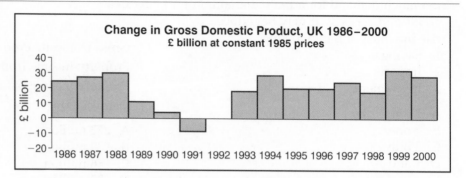

Change in Gross Domestic Product, UK 1986–2000
£ billion at constant 1985 prices

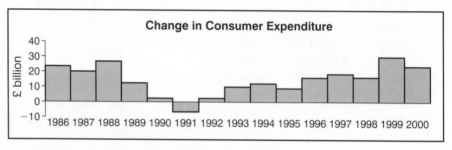

Change in Consumer Expenditure

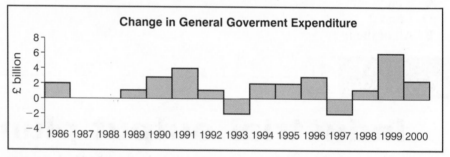

Change in General Goverment Expenditure

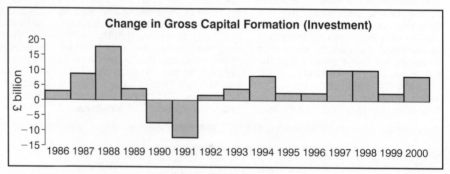

Change in Gross Capital Formation (Investment)

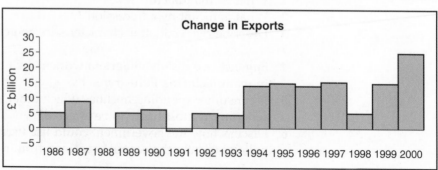

Change in Exports

Look at the graphs opposite which show movements in components of aggregate expenditure and Gross Domestic Product in the UK between 1986 and 2000.

1   What appears to be the most changeable component of aggregate expenditure? (2 marks)

2   Define what is meant by the following terms:
    a   Gross Domestic Product at market prices.
    b   Investment.
    c   Consumer expenditure.
    d   Aggregate demand. (8 marks)

3   Between 1990 and 1993 unemployment in the United Kingdom rose significantly. Explain one possible cause of this rise using information from the graph. (2 marks)

4   What evidence is there from the graph of the existence of a business cycle? (6 marks)

5   The following figures relate to the year 2000 as shown in the graphs above.

	£ billion (2000 prices)
Consumers' expenditure	539.0
General Government consumption	151.9
Investment	157.8
Exports	285.6
Imports	329.7

From the figures, calculate:
    a   Gross Final Expenditure.
    b   Gross Domestic Product. (4 marks)

6   The Government is presently trying to predict what will happen to output, employment and National Incomes in the United Kingdom in the next few years. Explain to them what could be the effect of each of the following factors.
    a   A rise in demand for imports.
    b   A rise in the amount consumers spend from their incomes.
    c   A rise in the demand for UK exports.
    d   A rise in taxation. (8 marks)

SUGGESTIONS FOR COURSEWORK

1   Consider the purchase of a product you have made recently at a local shop. Discuss in detail how you are creating output, employment and incomes for many more people in the economy. What role does the Government play in this circular flow? Is foreign trade involved? What effect would you, and people like you, have on the economy if you all stopped buying that product?

2   Examine the roles of your family in the circular flow of income in your economy as consumers, producers and citizens. How do they help create output, employment and income?

3   Investigate how has GDP has changed over the last 10–15 years in the UK or in your own country. What factors explain changes in the growth of GDP? Use data on consumer expenditure, public sector expenditure, investment and spending on exports and imports to compile charts and tables to illustrate the components of change in GDP. How have these changes affected employment in the economy? Is there evidence of a business cycle?

For UK data search the website of the Office of National Statistics (www.statistics.gov.uk) or look in one of the ONS publications *Economic Trends* or the *Annual Abstract of Statistics*.

Chapter 13

Macroeconomic problems (1): Inflation, Unemployment and Growth

Inflation refers to a sustained increase in the general level of prices of goods and services traded in an economy. That is, the prices of most goods and services available keep on rising.

Inflation is measured as a rate of increase in the general price level per period, usually every month and year. If the rate of price inflation is rising, prices are on average rising at a faster and faster rate. If inflation is falling, prices will still be rising but the rate of increase in prices will be slowing down.

The rate of inflation in an economy is measured by calculating the average price of a large sample of different goods and services on sale from many different businesses each month. As goods, services, and consumption patterns change over time, different goods, services, and places of sale will be added to the sample. Monthly or annual percentage changes in the average price of the sample of goods and services will usually be shown by the movement in a **price index**, with the average price set equal to 100 in the first month or year of measurement. In the UK the main measure of price inflation in the economy is the **Retail Prices Index** (RPI) which tracks the movement in the price of around 600 different goods and services sold at over 120 000 retail outlets each month.

Most economies hope to achieve low and stable inflation because high and rising inflation causes business uncertainty, reduces the price competitiveness of exports, and erodes the purchasing power of incomes. In turn this can lead to rising unemployment. Rising inflation may be caused by a combination of aggregate demand rising faster than supply, increasing production costs, and/or rising import prices because of a fall in the foreign exchange value of the currency.

Unemployment is a waste of productive resources. High levels of unemployment in an economy will tend to reduce income tax revenues and raise public expenditures on welfare benefits paid to those people out of work. In the UK unemployment is measured by the number of people claiming the **Jobseekers Allowance**. Cyclical unemployment will occur during an economic recession when aggregate demand for goods and services falls. **Structural unemployment** arises from longer term changes in the industrial structure of an economy. For example, during the early 1980s falling demand and a decline in many manufacturing industries in the UK increased labour unemployment to over 3 million people, or around 11% of the working population in the UK.

High inflation and unemployment in an economy can stifle **economic growth**. All economies aim to achieve economic growth in their total output and income. Growth is measured by the change per period of time in the real Gross Domestic Product of an economy. Economic growth tends to increase prosperity and raise living standards in an economy, but this may depend on how the benefits of growth are distributed between different groups and how growth is achieved. For example, if the population grows at a faster rate than output, then the average real GDP per head of the population will tend to fall. Similarly, producing more military goods and/or goods that release pollution during production may not improve overall living standards.

Economic growth can be achieved by employing previously unemployed resources, the discovery of new resources and more efficient production methods, better education and training, or by transferring existing resources from low-productivity uses to high-productivity uses.

MULTIPLE CHOICE

1 Which of the following are most likely to benefit when there is rapid inflation?

A Pensioners
B Borrowers
C Savers
D Consumers
E Workers

2 Which of the following is not a capital investment according to economists?

A Buying shares in a public limited company
B The building of a new road
C The purchase of new computer equipment by an office
D The construction of a new shopping centre
E Building a new oil pipeline

3 Which type of unemployment occurs when aggregate demand in an economy falls?

A Frictional
B Seasonal
C Voluntary
D Structural
E Cyclical

Questions 4 and 5 are based on the following table of statistics on selected economies for the year 2001:

Country	% Growth in Real GDP	% Change in Consumer Prices
Australia	3.7	5.1
Brazil	3.0	6.5
Taiwan	−1.9	0.3

4 Other things being equal, what clearly occurred in Brazil during 2001?

A Real GDP per head increased.
B Imported inflation.
C Economic growth.
D The standard of living fell.
E The purchasing power of money increased.

5 Which of the following statements does the table support?

A Price inflation fell in Taiwan.
B Real GDP growth was fastest in Brazil.
C Price inflation was stable in Australia.
D The Australian economy expanded faster than Brazil.
E Economic growth was slow in Taiwan.

(continued)

6   Demand-pull inflation may occur as a result of:

1   A rise in government spending.
2   A rise in demand for exports.
3   Falling investment.

A   1 only
B   2 only
C   3 only
D   1 and 2
E   All of them

7   Which of the following is least likely to be a cause of economic growth?

A   An increase in technical progress
B   An increase in training
C   An increase in capital investment
D   Improved education
E   An increase in taxation

8   Unemployment may arise as a result of which of the following reasons?

1   A fall in aggregate demand
2   High wage demands by unions
3   Reductions in employers' national insurance contributions for workers

A   1 only
B   2 only
C   3 only
D   1 and 2
E   All of them

9   Economic growth can be measured in terms of:

A   The increase in output every year.
B   The increase in national income every year.
C   The increase in GDP per head of the population each year.
D   The increase in real GDP per head of the population each year.
E   The increase in capital investment each year.

10   Study the following table.

Year	Inflation	Increase in wages (average)
1	7%	12%
2	10%	13.2%
3	16.4%	10.1%
4	12%	13%
5	9.2%	19%

In which year was there the largest increase in real wages?

A   Year 1
B   Year 2
C   Year 3
D   Year 4
E   Year 5

11   All of the following may cause cost push inflation *except*:

A   An increase in wages.
B   An increase in rent.
C   An increase in oil prices.
D   An increase in consumer expenditure.
E   An increase in import prices.

12

Item	Price index	Weight
Food	120	50
Housing	130	40
Services	110	10
	All items =	100

What is the weighted price index for all items?

A   360
B   123
C   120
D   100
E   125

The tables below provide economic data on inflation, unemployment and economic growth in three major economies between 1986 and 2001.

Canada	1986–1989	1990–1993	1994–1997	1998–2001
Average annual % change in real GDP	3.5	0.4	3.3	3.3
Average annual % change in consumer price index	4.2	4.2	1.4	1.7
Unemployment as a % of workforce	8.4	10.3	9.7	7.9

Japan	1986–1989	1990–1993	1994–1997	1998–2001
Average annual % change in real GDP	4.5	2.6	2.2	0.5
Average annual % change in consumer price index	0.5	2.6	0.6	−0.2
Unemployment as a % of workforce	2.6	2.2	3.2	4.6

United Kingdom	1986–1989	1990–1993	1994–1997	1998–2001
Average annual % change in real GDP	4.0	0.4	3.3	2.5
Average annual % change in consumer price index	4.1	6.7	2.9	2.3
Unemployment as a % of workforce	9.0	8.7	8.2	6.1

Source: *OECD 'World Economic Outlook', 2001*

1 What does 'GDP' stand for and what does it mean? (2 marks)
2 Explain the difference between real GDP and nominal or money GDP. (2 marks)
3 Why is it important for an economy to grow real GDP? (4 marks)
4 From the table, which economy experienced
   a the largest percentage growth in real GDP 1990–1993, and
   b the lowest percentage growth in real GDP 1998–2001? (4 marks)
5 What is the difference between cyclical and structural unemployment? (4 marks)
6 What evidence, if any, does the table provide to suggest the major economies experienced cyclical unemployment during the early 1990s? (Would you expect a relationship between these two economic variables and why?) (6 marks)
7 Which economy has experienced price deflation? What economic problems do you think are associated with prolonged price deflation? (6 marks)
8 What, if anything, does the table suggest about the relationship between the rate of unemployment and price inflation? (6 marks)

'South Africa is in pursuit of higher economic growth to make it a leading emerging market. Having laid the foundations of a stable macroeconomic environment, including the lowering of price inflation, the government is now seeking to attract increased levels of foreign direct investment and strengthening trade ties with its partners.'

Year	% change in consumer price index	% change in Real GDP
1996	8.7	4.2
1997	7.0	2.5
1998	6.9	0.5
1999	5.2	1.9
2000	5.4	3.1
2001	5.9	2.3

Adapted from *FT Country Surveys, South Africa 1999, 2000*

1   What is 'economic growth' and how is it measured?   (4 marks)
2   What is 'inflation'?   (2 marks)
3   Describe how price inflation can be measured.   (4 marks)
4   Explain the different causes of demand-pull inflation and
    cost-push inflation.   (4 marks)
5   Using the information in the table describe the economic
    performance of South Africa over the period 1996–2001   (6 marks)
6   Explain economic reasons why the South African government
    has been 'in pursuit of higher economic growth' and lower
    price inflation.   (6 marks)

Retail Prices Index, UK 1987–2001

1987	100
1988	106.9
1989	115.2
1990	126.1
1991	133.5
1992	138.5
1993	140.7
1994	144.1
1995	149.1
1996	152.7
1997	157.5
1998	162.9
1999	165.4
2000	170.3
2001	173.1

The above table presents data on the UK Retail Prices Index at the end of each year between 1987 and 2001. Changes in the RPI provide information on the rate of price inflation in the UK.

1 What is 'price inflation'? (2 marks)
2 Suggest why governments collect statistics to measure price inflation in their economies. (4 marks)
3 In which year in the table was the rate of increase in price inflation in the UK at its highest, and in which year was the rate of increase at its lowest? (4 marks)
4 Explain why a 10% increase in the average price of food products in the UK is unlikely to increase the RPI by 10%. (4 marks)
5 What would the RPI be for 2002 be if, on average, the prices of goods and services used to calculate the UK price index increase by 2.6% that year? Show your calculations. (6 marks)

SUGGESTIONS FOR COURSEWORK

1 Conduct a survey of prices of a number of goods at different shops in your area. Visit the shops regularly over a number of weeks. Each week calculate the average price of all the goods and express them in a price index. Compare your price index with the increase in the general price index for your economy over the same period.

Assess how the price changes you have noted may affect different households, for example, a pensioner household, unemployed people, one parent families.

2 If you can, visit a local factory and try to find out how they arrive at the final price they sell their product for. Is there evidence of cost plus profit pricing? Or are they determined by the forces of demand and supply? Try to find out what has caused their prices to rise over the past few years, if indeed they have risen. Describe your findings and try to decide to what extent they support the view that inflation is cost push or the view that it is caused by increasing demand.

3 Conduct an interview with a number of different unemployed people you know. Try to find out why they are unemployed and the personal costs they face. What benefits do they receive? Do you think they are adequate? Write up your findings in a report on the costs of unemployment to the economy.

4 Write a report to the Government expressing your concern about the plight of less developed countries. Outline the policies you would use to help them achieve economic growth.

Chapter 14

Macroeconomic problems (2): International Trade

Countries will trade with each other to obtain goods and services they cannot produce themselves, or they can only produce at a higher cost. Countries will specialize in the production of commodities in which they have a **comparative advantage**. That is, they will produce goods and services they can do so most efficiently and then trade to obtain a greater variety of commodities.

Visible trade involves trade in physical commodities while **invisible trade** involves the exchange of services. **Exports** are represented by flows of money coming into a country in payment for goods and services sold overseas. **Imports** are represented by money flowing out of a country to pay for foreign goods and services. The **balance of trade** shows the difference between the value of visible exports and imports. A favourable trade balance means the value of visible exports from a country exceeds the value of its visible imports.

The **balance of payments** of a country records all the payments it has made for imports and all its receipts from sales of exports. The balance of payments is usually split into three main sections. The **current account** measures how well the country is doing in trade in goods and services. The **capital account** records flows of money into and out of the country to pay for transfers of assets to and from overseas by migrant firms and workers, and also includes foreign aids. The **financial account** records flows of money into and out of the country to pay for investments in capital, shares and loans. Any profits, dividends and interest payments (IPD) resulting from these investments will usually be recorded in the current account.

When countries trade commodities they must also trade their foreign currencies in order to be able to pay each other in their own money. The **foreign exchange rate** of a currency is its price in terms of other currencies. Like all other commodities the price of a currency is determined by the forces of demand and supply. An increase in the demand for a foreign currency and/or a fall in its supply will cause its value in terms of other currencies to appreciate while a fall in demand for the currency and/or a rise in its supply will cause its value to depreciate. However, many countries have in the past, or continue to, fix their exchange rates. A devaluation of a fixed exchange rate may be necessary for a country when the value of the currency is too high, causing export prices to appear uncompetitive against import prices thereby resulting in trade deficits. Sometimes countries will introduce trade barriers to correct a deficit and/or protect their domestic firms from competition from imported goods and services.

1 The following table shows the output of two countries before specialization with each country dividing up their resources equally between the production of two goods.

	Good X	Good Y
Country A	100	50
Country B	60	40

Consider each of the following statements.
1 Country A has an absolute advantage in X and Y.
2 Both countries would benefit from specialization and trade.
3 Country B has the comparative advantage in the production of Good Y.

Which of them are true?

A 1 only
B 2 only
C 3 only
D 1 and 2
E All of them

2 Which of the following policies is unlikely to correct a balance of payments deficit?

A A rise in income tax to reduce consumer spending
B An embargo on imported goods
C A lowering of interest rates
D A devaluation of the currency
E Tariffs on imports

3 If the value of $1 on the foreign exchange market were 1.25 euros, how much would a car that sells for 20 000 euros in Germany sell for in the USA if transport costs and tariffs were zero?

A $25 000
B $16 000
C $12 500
D $20 000
E $18 000

4 Which of the following situations is likely to lead to an appreciation in the value of the US dollar?
1 A rise in interest rates to attract hot money
2 A rise in demand for US exports
3 A balance of payments deficit

A 1 only
B 2 only
C 3 only
D 1 and 2
E All of them

5 Which of the following could be used to restrict imports?
1 Quota
2 Embargo
3 Tighter safety regulations

A 1 only
B 2 only
C 3 only
D 1 and 2
E All of them

6 Which of the following act as barriers against free trade?
1 Tariffs
2 Embargoes
3 Devaluation

A 1 only
B 2 only
C 3 only
D 1 and 2
E All of them

7 A country has a visible trade deficit of $5bn and a surplus of invisible trade of $12bn. This means the country has

A A balance of payments surplus.
B A favourable balance of trade.
C A surplus on capital account.
D A current account surplus.
E A deficit on the financial account.

8 Which of the following is an invisible export of Mauritius?

   A A resident of Mauritius visiting Europe
   B Dividends paid by a company in Mauritius to overseas shareholders
   C A loan to Mauritius from France
   D Loan interest payments to France
   E Sales of Japanese cars in Mauritius

9 Which of the following factors explains international trade in manufactured goods?

   A Different national laws and regulations
   B High tariff barriers between countries
   C Trade embargos between countries
   D High transport costs to different countries
   E Different production costs between countries

10 Which of the following is an invisible import to the UK?

   A A German car
   B A Japanese tourist
   C An Italian bottle of wine
   D A loan of money to Spain
   E A loan of money from France

11 In 1998 the value of the UK pound increased in value by 10% against the US dollar. What was the most likely reason for this?

   A Speculative buying of US dollars
   B Rising inflation in the UK
   C Higher interest rates in the UK than in the US
   D A fall in the demand for UK exports
   E An increase in demand for US exports

12 Which of the following transactions will be recorded in the financial account of the balance of payments of Jamaica?

   A Spending by US tourists visiting Jamaica
   B Spending by Jamaican tourists in the USA
   C The purchase of a Jamaican company by a Japanese company
   D Dividends paid to Japanese shareholders in a Jamaican company
   E The earnings of Jamaicans working overseas

DATA RESPONSE 1

'Hi-tech consumer electronic goods produced in Japan, such as DVD players and digital camcorders, are sold into markets all over the world. The high price elasticity of many of these items has resulted in a significant increase in demand for them as their prices continue to fall in real terms.'

1 Why do some countries import consumer electronic goods from Japan despite having the capability to manufacture similar products themselves?   (6 marks)

2 How will sales of consumer electronic goods by Japan be classified in the balance of payments of Japan and the other countries that purchase them?   (4 marks)

3 What effect could rising demand for imports from Japan have on the value of the Japanese currency, the Yen? Show this effect using a suitable diagram.   (6 marks)

4 Explain the term 'high price elasticity of demand'.   (4 marks)

5 How could knowledge of the price elasticity of demand for different goods and services overseas help exporting companies?   (4 marks)

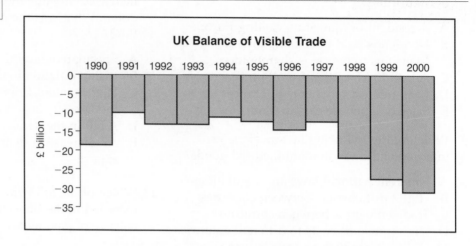

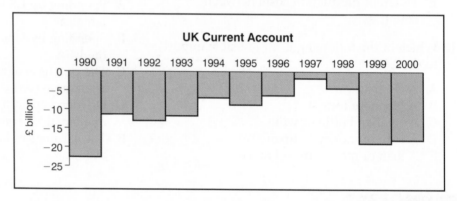

1 Suggest two reasons why countries trade. (4 marks)
2 Explain what the balance of payments on current account records. (2 marks)
3 Why are governments interested in the balance of payments? (4 marks)
4 Use examples to distinguish between a visible export and an invisible export. (4 marks)
5 Compare the changes in the current account balance with the balance of visible trade between 1990 and 2000. (4 marks)
6 Suggest two factors that might explain successive deficits in the UK trade balance. (6 marks)
7 Explain what effect the following factors might have on the UK balance of payments current account:
   a a rise in UK interest rates
   b a rise in UK inflation
   c a fall in the value of the UK currency (12 marks)

US imposes 30% tariffs on steel imports

Yesterday the US imposed 30 per cent tariffs on most steel imports to protect a domestic industry that says it has been battered by imports of cheap steel. The trade restrictions are the most severe ever imposed by the US on steel, going well beyond the mid-1980s when the US forced Europe and Japan to curb steel exports to the US or face punishing quotas.

The European Union pledged to launch a complaint to the World Trade Organization against the new US steel tariffs, which it said represented 'a clear violation of WTO rules on free trade'.

The EU, which supplies about one-fifth of US steel imports, is likely to be hardest hit by the US actions. Corus, the Anglo-Dutch steel group, warned they would have a 'potentially harmful' effect on its business.

In a hard-hitting statement, Pascal Lamy, the EU trade commissioner, said the EU would take whatever measures necessary to protect its steel industry from an expected surge in imports as other steelmakers accustomed to exporting to the US, such as Russia, Japan and South Korea, search for alternative markets.

'I fear the US move will end any hope of finding an internationally agreed solution to overcapacity problems faced by the world steel industry, and will not rein in global subsidies' Mr Lamy said. Talks were supposed to resume next month in Paris to look for negotiated cuts in global steel output.

Adapted from *The Financial Times, 6.3.2002*

1 Suggest reasons why the US imports steel from other countries as well as having US companies able to produce steel. (4 marks)
2 What is a 'tariff'? How does it differ from a 'quota'? (4 marks)
3 Why do you think the US imposed a tariff on steel imports? (6 marks)
4 Suggest why the World Trade Organization might consider the US tariff a 'violation of WTO rules on free trade'. (4 marks)
5 Suggest why subsidies given by various governments to their domestic steel industries could have resulted in 'overcapacity problems faced by the world steel industry'. (6 marks)
6 Explain the possible impact the US tariff could have on the output and employment of steel companies in other countries. (6 marks)
7 Discuss the effects that a rise in the value of the US dollar might have on the US economy (including the balance of payments, price inflation, employment and economic growth). (8 marks)

SUGGESTIONS FOR COURSEWORK

1 Investigate a trade dispute between any two countries or groups of countries. Examine the reasons for the dispute. What impact will the dispute have on the industries and economies involved in the dispute? How will/has the dispute been resolved, and what effects will this have? A list of current disputes and rulings by the World Trade Organization is available on-line at www.wto.org under 'disputes'.

2   In which industries does your country have a comparative advantage? What are its major exports and imports? Investigate the reasons for the comparative advantage(s) of your country, and how it affects the pattern of international trade between your country and others. How has this changed over time and why?

3   Track the value of the exchange rate of your national currency against other major world currencies, such as the US dollar, the Japanese Yen, UK Sterling, and the euro. Use business newspapers such as *The Financial Times* or Internet websites for exchange rates to find out this information. Plot the movements in your exchange rate each day or weekly and investigate why these changes have occurred.

Chapter 15 | Controlling the Macroeconomy

Government policy in most developed economies has four main **macroeconomic objectives**:

- to achieve low and stable price inflation
- to maintain a high level of employment
- to encourage economic growth
- to encourage trade and secure a favourable balance of payments.

In order to achieve these objectives a government will attempt to influence the demand side and supply side of their macroeconomy. The **aggregate demand** in an economy is the total demand for all goods and services by consumers, firms and government organizations. The **aggregate supply** is the total supply of all goods and services to the economy. These can be goods and services produced domestically or imported from overseas.

If aggregate demand increases rapidly in an economy, for example, due to a consumer spending boom, it may cause a demand-push inflation if the aggregate supply of goods and services is unable to expand at the same rate. **Demand-side policies** will aim to reduce the growth in aggregate demand. **Fiscal policy** may be used to raise taxes and/or reduce government expenditure. Alternatively, or at the same time, **monetary policy** can be used to raise interest rates. This will make borrowing money more expensive for consumers and firms. Higher interest rates will also tend to increase the value of the currency on the foreign exchange market. This will help to reduce the price of imported goods.

During a recession, aggregate demand, output and employment will all tend to fall. Fiscal policy may be used to boost aggregate demand by cutting taxes and/or increasing government spending on goods and services. Monetary policy may help to boost demand by lowering interest rates.

In the UK, the base rate of interest in the economy is set each month by the **Monetary Policy Committee**. The MPC is a panel of economists who base their decision on interest rates using up to date information on the state of the UK economy. If they think the economy is 'overheating' (aggregate demand is rising too fast), they will tend to increase the interest rate charged by the **Bank of England** to the banking system. The Governor of the Bank of England is head of the MPC.

Supply-side policies help to stimulate economic growth in the aggregate supply of goods and services. If the national output can be increased to satisfy growing aggregate demand, then general price inflation can be kept low. Supply-side policies will attempt to remove any barriers to growth in aggregate supply. For example, reducing the burden of income tax may encourage more people into work and other workers to work harder. Lowering taxes on company profits may encourage more firms to invest and expand. **Competition policy** curbs the market power of some very large firms, or groups of firms, who may try to boost their profits by restricting market supply in order to force up prices charged to consumers. **Deregulation** may involve removing old and unnecessary laws and regulations on businesses for example, by doing away with restrictions on shop opening hours, allowing public services to be provided by private firms (**privatization**), and cutting bureaucracy.

MULTIPLE CHOICE

1 Which of the following measures would not be used in fiscal policy?

   A Reducing income tax
   B Increasing spending on roads
   C Increasing interest rates
   D Reducing VAT
   E Increasing the budget deficit

2 Expansionary fiscal policy to increase aggregate demand involves:

   A Increasing the money supply and reducing interest rates.
   B Increasing public spending and taxes.
   C Reducing public spending and taxes.
   D Reducing interest rates and the money supply.
   E Increasing public spending and reducing taxes.

3 Monetary policy involves control of:
   1 Interest rates.
   2 The supply of money.
   3 The level of aggregate demand.

   A 1 only
   B 2 only
   C 3 only
   D 1 and 2
   E All of them

4 An increase in the money supply may:
   1 Lower interest rates.
   2 Increase consumer borrowing.
   3 Increase inflation.

   A 1 only
   B 2 only
   C 3 only
   D 1 and 2
   E All of them

5 A government can reduce the supply of money by all of the following except:

   A Calling for special deposits.

   B Reduced government borrowing from banks.
   C Selling bonds to the general public.
   D Reducing taxes.
   E Asking the banks to reduce their lending.

6 In the coming year consumers are expected to save more of their incomes. If the government doesn't want national income to fall it should:

   A Increase interest rates.
   B Increase its own expenditure.
   C Reduce the budget deficit.
   D Redistribute income from the rich to the poor.
   E Cut tariffs.

7 To increase demand in a developed economy a government could try to:

   A Reduce road building.
   B Cut subsidies to industry.
   C Encourage savings.
   D Budget for a surplus.
   E Cut taxes.

8 Which of the following functions is performed by a Central Bank but not a commercial bank?

   A Making loans
   B Holding deposits
   C Controlling the money supply
   D Changing foreign currencies
   E Giving financial advice

9 A government wishes to reduce total consumer spending in an economy. What should it increase?

   A Government expenditure
   B Value Added Tax
   C Interest rates
   D The minimum wage
   E Public sector pay

(continued)

Questions 10–14 refer to the following instruments of economic policy:

A Reducing taxes on company profits
B Increasing the interest rate
C Raising welfare benefits
D Increasing fines on businesses found guilty of operating cartels
E Increasing income taxes

Which of the above instruments best describes the following government actions:

10 A fiscal measure to reduce growth in consumer spending?

11 Tightening monetary policy to reduce consumer demand?

12 A supply side measure to encourage businesses to invest and expand output?

13 A fiscal policy expansion to encourage economic growth?

14 Competition policy?

DATA RESPONSE *1*

Rates soar as inflation rears its head

The base rate of interest will rise to 5.5% from their present 4%, City analysts predict. And some see the first hike coming as early as next month.

Fear of a rapid climb in rates has been stoked by last week's shock jump in underlying inflation from 1.9% to 2.6%, above the Government's 2.5% target. It is likely to be compounded by retail sales figures out on Thursday. They should show that the consumer boom continued in January, with sales volumes up about 6% on a year earlier.

Adapted from *The Sunday Times, 3.2.2002*

1 What is inflation? Suggest two reasons why the Government wants to control rising inflation. (6 marks)

2 What is meant by the 'base rate of interest'? (2 marks)

3 Explain how an increase in the base rate can help to curb rising price inflation. (4 marks)

4 What impact could higher interest rates have on capital investment in the economy and economic growth? Explain your answer. (6 marks)

5 Suggest other policies the UK Government could use in an attempt to reduce inflation. (8 marks)

Banks cut rates over rising fears of recession

Europe's leading central banks yesterday emulated the US Federal Reserve and cut interest rates by half a percentage point in an effort to avert a global recession.

The Bank of England lowered its principal interest rate to 4 per cent while the European Central Bank reduced its main lending rate to 3.25 per cent.

The decision, swiftly matched by almost all large mortgage lenders, was the Bank's first half-point cut in more than two years. It followed a similar move by the US Federal Reserve on Tuesday and was echoed yesterday by the European Central Bank. However, Wim Duisenberg, ECB president, denied the three cuts were co-ordinated.

With recent data showing UK economic growth close to trend, in contrast to the US and eurozone, yesterday's Bank cut showed a determination to pre-empt the slowdown rather than waiting for cast-iron proof of its arrival.

Bridget Rosewell, chief economic adviser to the British Retail Consortium, said a quarter-point cut would probably have been enough to keep consumer spending solid. But she said that other parts of the economy – notably business investment – needed more help, and warned that rising unemployment would damage consumer confidence.

The Bank and ECB gave similar reasons for their decisions.

Mr Duisenberg said: 'Confidence has been harder hit than we thought only a few weeks ago.' He warned that new forecasts suggested the recovery in the eurozone economy would be postponed. A Bank statement said surveys of UK confidence and business activity were showing weakness and price pressures were subdued.

UK business leaders welcomed the decision, though both the British Chambers of Commerce and the Engineering Employers' Federation said that manufacturers would need extra help from Gordon Brown, the chancellor, in the pre-Budget report.

Adapted from *The Financial Times, 9.11.2001*

1 Describe the main economic characteristics of a recession.   (4 marks)
2 What is 'monetary policy'?   (4 marks)
3 Explain how cutting interest rates might help 'avert a global recession'.   (4 marks)
4 Suggest other policies a government might use to raise aggregate demand in an economy to help promote an economic recovery.   (6 marks)
5 Describe two other functions of a central bank like the Bank of England in the UK or the European Central Bank in the European Union.   (4 marks)

SUGGESTIONS FOR COURSEWORK

1 Examine the main economic policies of your present government. What are its main economic objectives? Describe its policies and analyse their effects on consumers, producers and citizens.

2 Imagine a group of you are the government of a country with the following characteristics:

- Small size near Europe
- Few natural resources
- Many highly skilled workers
- High unemployment
- Low inflation
- Many imports
- High wage demands
- General election this year
- Poor production levels
- Low level of investment in firms
- Average level of taxes
- Heavy reliance on exports
- Balance of payments recently gone into deficit
- Grows half the food it needs

Below are some economic policies your government could use to manage your economy. Choose six policies and write down why you have chosen these particular policies and what effect you hope they will have on the economy of your country.

1 Privatizing many public services.
2 Increasing all taxes.
3 Cutting government spending.
4 Providing money for research into new production methods.
5 Helping move firms to regions of high unemployment.
6 Lowering interest rates to encourage borrowing.
7 Reducing the value of your currency.
8 Increasing aid to underdeveloped countries.
9 Giving grants to firms to help them employ more workers.
10 Increasing government borrowing.
11 Increasing taxes on foreign firms in your country.
12 Encouraging people to invest in domestic firms.
13 Increasing interest rates to discourage borrowing.
14 Reducing taxes on profits to encourage foreign firms to your country.
15 Raising the value of your currency.
16 Reducing all taxes.
17 Increasing spending on schools, hospitals, pensions, etc.
18 Reducing government borrowing.
19 Increasing business supports for training schemes.
20 Placing tariffs on all imports.
21 Cutting welfare benefits.
22 Passing laws to outlaw restrictive practices.
23 Increasing 'green' taxes to reduce pollution.
24 Introducing a minimum wage for low-paid workers.
25 Cutting subsidies paid to large farms.

Chapter 16 | How is Government Financed?

The **public sector** in a country consists of organizations funded by or accountable to local and central government. Public sector organizations can provide many goods and services either because the private sector is unwilling or unable to provide in sufficient quantity or quality. For example, the public sector will provide public goods, such as street lighting and defence, because private sector firms would find it difficult to charge people for them according to their usage. **Merit goods** are thought by government to be good for people and the economy to have, regardless of their ability to pay for them, and will include education, police and fire services, and roads. The public sector may also provide many **public and social services**, such as subsidised passenger rail services, care for the elderly, and disability benefits.

Each year the public sector in many countries will spend a large amount of money on the provision of goods and services, and collects revenue to pay for this spending, principally from taxes. In this way, the government of a country can also influence the level of aggregate demand and output in the economy through **fiscal policy**.

The **current expenditure** of a government includes wages paid to public sector workers, welfare benefits for the unemployed, disabled and old age pensioners, and on consumer goods. **Capital expenditure** will include public sector investments in new roads, schools, hospitals and defence equipment.

Direct taxes, are levied on incomes, company profits, and wealth. Indirect taxes are levied on expenditure, through additional charges on the price of many goods and services. **Indirect taxes** include Value Added Tax (VAT), other sales taxes and excise duties – for example on alcohol, fuel and tobacco. In addition to national taxes, local authorities may raise money to help pay for their spending through local taxes, for example from charges on business and residential properties. In some countries, sales taxes may also vary locally.

A **budget** is a plan for government spending and tax revenue in the forthcoming year. Each year a government will announce its aims for the economy and how it intends to achieve these through plans for the level and pattern of public spending and taxation. If planned government spending exceeds forecast tax revenues, the budget is said to be **in deficit**. If planned spending is less than forecast tax revenues the budget will be **in surplus**. The **public sector net borrowing requirement** is a measure of how much government will have to borrow in a year if general government spending is less than total tax and other revenues. If the net borrowing requirement is negative, it means the government has received more in revenue in a year than it has spent in total, and it can therefore use the surplus of revenue to repay some of the national debt. The **national debt** is the total stock of public sector borrowing accumulated over time. Annual interest payments on the national debt are included in annual public sector expenditure.

1 Which of the following is an indirect tax?

   A A tax on inherited wealth
   B A tax on consumer goods and services
   C A tax on company profits
   D A tax on income from employment
   E A tax on interest earned in savings

2 John Smith earns £12 000 per year and pays £3000 in income tax. Mary Brown earns £18 000 per year and pays £6000 in income tax. This income tax is:

   A Proportional
   B Regressive
   C Progressive
   D A poll tax
   E Indirect

3 The following are a government's receipts from taxation.

	£ million
VAT	400
Corporation tax	200
Excise duties	100
Income tax	750
Capital gains tax	250

   What is the total amount of indirect tax revenue?
   A £950 m   C £500 m   E £150 m
   B £400 m   D £700 m

4 In which of the following situations will there be a budget deficit?

   A Government spending exceeds government revenue.
   B Government revenue exceeds government spending.
   C Government spending exceeds total tax revenue.
   D Government spending exceeds direct tax revenues.
   E Government spending exceeds indirect tax revenues.

5 The use of taxation and government spending to influence the economy is known as:

   A Regional policy.
   B Monetary policy.
   C Competition policy.
   D Trade policy.
   E Fiscal policy.

6 The national debt of a country is

   A The total amount of public spending.
   B The budget deficit.
   C The annual public sector borrowing requirement.
   D The total stock of public and private sector borrowing.
   E The total accumulated stock of public sector borrowing.

7 Which of the following is not included in public expenditure?

   A Subsidies to rail companies from central government
   B Wages paid to public sector employees
   C Interest payments on local authority borrowing
   D Capital investments by public limited companies
   E Investments in roads by central government

Questions 8–10 are based on the following table of information on taxes paid on different levels of income under different tax systems (A–E).

| Weekly income | Tax paid from income £ | | | | |
£	A	B	C	D	E
150	30	30	15	40	45
200	40	60	20	40	50
400	50	150	40	40	55

Which of the tax systems in the table is

8 the most progressive?

9 the most regressive?

10 proportional?

11 Which of the following is a direct tax?

   A VAT
   B Fuel duties
   C Tobacco duties
   D Air passenger tax
   E Income tax

(continued)

12 The following table shows public spending and revenues in a country.

Year	Public Expenditure ($ billion)	Total Revenue ($ billion)
2	90	80
3	110	95
4	140	135

If the national debt of a country is $100 billion in year 1, what will be the size of the national debt in year 3 if no debt has been repaid?

A $5 billion
B $100 billion
C $30 billion
D $130 billion
E $70 billion

13 A good tax system should:
1 Be understandable.
2 Be cheap to administer.
3 Not discourage working.

A 1 only
B 2 only
C 3 only
D 1 and 2
E All of them

14 A government may spend money for which of the following reasons?
1 To provide merit goods
2 To redistribute income
3 To influence the level of demand in the economy

A 1 only
B 2 only
C 3 only
D 1 and 2
E All of them

DATA RESPONSE 1

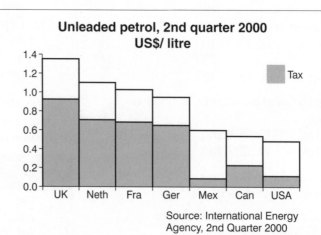

Unleaded petrol, 2nd quarter 2000 US$/ litre

Source: International Energy Agency, 2nd Quarter 2000

Fuel is taxed at various different stages in the process of turning crude oil into petrol, and the amount of tax depends on each government's polices.

In the US, tax accounts for 22% of the cost of a litre of petrol, while in the UK – the highest fuel-taxing country, it accounts for almost 73%.

British drivers pay two taxes on the petrol they buy at the pump: fuel duty and VAT. Of these, fuel duty remains by far the most significant – and remains the most controversial. According to figures released with the 2000 Budget, the UK Government forecasts that revenue from fuel duties will continue to rise rapidly from £21.6bn in the 1998–99 financial year to £23.3bn by the end of the 2000–01 financial year.

Adapted from *BBC News Online, 21.9.2000*

1 Suggest two reasons why governments impose taxes on petrol. (4 marks)
2 What is the difference between an excise duty, such as Fuel Duty, and Value Added Tax (VAT)? (4 marks)
3 Taxes on expenditure, such as Fuel Duty and VAT, are argued to be 'regressive'. What does this mean? (4 marks)
4 Petrol and cars are complementary goods. Explain what this means, and describe how the difference in petrol prices in the UK and USA may affect their joint demand in these countries. (6 marks)
5 Using petrol as an example, explain how knowledge of the price elasticity of demand for different goods and services can help a government decide which taxes to raise **a** to reduce consumption, and **b** for the purpose of raising revenue. (8 marks)

DATA RESPONSE 2

UK public spending and receipts, 2001-02

Where taxpayers' money is spent

Total managed expenditure £394 billion

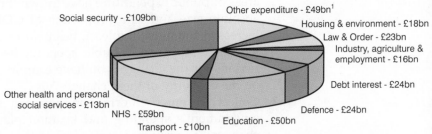

Social security - £109bn
Other expenditure - £49bn[1]
Housing & environment - £18bn
Law & Order - £23bn
Industry, agriculture & employment - £16bn
Debt interest - £24bn
Defence - £24bn
Education - £50bn
Transport - £10bn
NHS - £59bn
Other health and personal social services - £13bn

[1] includes spending on central adminisration, culture, media and sport, international cooperation and developement and public service pensions plus spending yet to be allocated and some accounting adjustments

Where taxes come from

Total receipts £398 billion

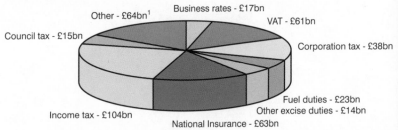

Other - £64bn[1]
Business rates - £17bn
VAT - £61bn
Corporation tax - £38bn
Council tax - £15bn
Fuel duties - £23bn
Other excise duties - £14bn
Income tax - £104bn
National Insurance - £63bn

[1] includes capital gains tax, inheritance tax, stamp duties, vehicle excise duties and some other tax and non-tax reciepts (e.g. interest and dividends).

Source: HM Treasury, 2001–02 figures following Budget 2001

1   Provide three reasons why governments intervene in market economies through public spending and taxation policies.   (6 marks)

2   According to the charts, **a** which tax raised the most revenue and **b** what was the largest public expenditure commitment, in the UK in the financial year 2001–02?   (4 marks)

3   What is the difference between a 'direct' tax and an 'indirect' tax?   (4 marks)

4   From the charts identify and list two direct taxes and two indirect taxes.   (4 marks)

5   Was the Budget in deficit or in surplus in the UK in 2001–02? (4 marks)

6   What is 'fiscal policy'?   (4 marks)

7   Discuss the possible effects on the UK economy if the UK Government were to budget for an increased deficit in future years (for example, on price inflation, employment, output and trade).   (8 marks)

SUGGESTIONS FOR COURSEWORK

1   Investigate how the amount and pattern of public expenditures and taxation in your country has changed over the last 5–10 years. Which areas of public expenditure have grown the most, the least, or fallen (in absolute size and as a proportion of GDP)? Which taxes have been increased the most, the least, been cut or done away with? Have any new taxes and areas of public spending been introduced? What are the reasons for the changes you have examined? What has been the effect on the economy of these changes?

2   Collect as much information you can on your national or local government's spending and taxation plans for the next year. What changes are proposed and why? Is the government budgeting for a deficit or surplus? What do you think are the likely effects of these changes on your national, or local, economy?

Chapter 17 | The Distribution of Income and Wealth

The distribution of income and wealth is about how goods and services in an economy are shared out among people.

Anything owned by people with a money value is wealth, for example, machinery or housing. A nation's wealth is measured as the stock of things of value in a country at a particular moment in time.

All of the physical goods and financial assets in a country are known as that country's **non-human** wealth. Nations also possess **human wealth** – that is, the education, training, skills and work experience of their people.

While wealth can be measured as the stock of things of value in a country at a certain point in time, income can only be measured over time. For example, income is earnings per week or month – that is, income is a flow of earnings over time.

Income is earned from both human and non-human wealth. For example, a doctor will earn a high income because of the large amount of training or human wealth that she possesses. Less skilled workers will have a smaller amount of human wealth and are more likely to earn smaller incomes. Incomes are also earned from non-human wealth such as bank or building society accounts.

The **distribution of wealth** refers to how the stock of wealth in an economy is shared out between people. Individuals or families may accumulate wealth at different rates due to success in business or work, differences in incomes and savings rates, or by pure luck such as winning the lottery. Differences in wealth may continue from generation to generation because wealth is passed on through inheritance. Inequality in the distribution of wealth may be reduced through wealth and inheritance taxes. Similarly, progressively higher rates of tax on incomes may help to reduce income inequalities between those in work, while welfare benefits may be paid to the poor and those on low incomes or unable to work.

The distribution of both incomes and wealth between people is unequal in all countries, and unequal between different countries. Large differences in incomes between countries often reflect their different stages of development. Less developed countries in the world may suffer from high population growth, a lack of trained workers, poor transport and communications and a lack of capital investment. These factors tend to be both the cause and effect of slow economic growth in the national income and output.

1 Which of the following is/are true?
1. Wealth is more evenly distributed than income.
2. Wealth is more difficult to measure than income.
3. Wealth is more heavily taxed than income.

   A 1 only
   B 2 only
   C 3 only
   D 1 and 2
   E All of them

2 Which of the following can be classed as unearned income?

   A The monthly salary of an accountant
   B The weekly wages of a chemist
   C The monthly interest on a deposit account
   D The lump sum payment as an advance on royalties for an author
   E The commission received by sales agents

3 Which of the following would lead to a more unequal distribution of income?
1. A cut in unemployment benefits
2. A cut in taxes on profit
3. An increase in old age pensions

   A 1 only
   B 2 only
   C 3 only
   D 1 and 2
   E All of them

4 Which of the following countries has the greatest GDP per capita?

Country	Population	GDP ($M)
A	1000	10 000
B	700	9 000
C	1500	16 000
D	1900	21 000
E	2400	14 800

DATA RESPONSE 1

Country	GDP (US $ millions)	Population (millions)
India	414 010	970.9
Paraguay	8 505	5.2
Spain	582 138	39.6
Turkey	198 007	63.5

Source: *United Nations Statistical Yearbook 2001*

1 What is GDP? Explain why is it important for GDP to grow. (3 marks)

2 Calculate GDP per head in each of the above countries. (4 marks)

3 Which of the above countries has the highest GDP per head? (1 mark)

4 What will be the effect on GDP per head in a country if population rises at a faster rate than economic growth? (2 marks)

5 What other information would be useful to compare the general standard of living and level of development in the above countries? (6 marks)

6 Discuss how a government could use fiscal policy to help people on low incomes through changes in public expenditures and taxation. (8 marks)

Even billionaires face a dose of economic pain

The world's billionaires lost 11 per cent of their wealth last year, and 83 people fell out of the billionaire club altogether, according to the latest survey from Forbes.

The magazine's 2002 survey of the world's richest people counts 497 with net worth of more than $1bn. Only 23 per cent saw their fortunes climb last year, while half lost money.

Bill Gates, chairman of computer giant Microsoft, was one loser, shedding $6bn in the last nine months, but easily kept his place at the top of the billionaire pile with $52.8bn.

But plummeting stock prices took a heavy toll on other technology and media executives. Ted Turner, vice-chairman of media group AOL Time Warner, who was worth $8.8bn in 2001, dropped $5bn and more than 60 places. But the biggest loser was Leo Kirch, the German media magnate, whose estimated fortune dwindled from $12bn to just $1bn.

There were some success stories, however. Warren Buffett, the investment guru who refused to join in the internet stock boom, saw his fortune rise $2.4bn to $35bn, despite terrorism-related insurance losses in his Berkshire Hathaway group. He retained his No. 2 spot on the rich list, behind Mr Gates.

Retailers also had a good year. Karl and Theo Albrecht, the German brothers whose Aldi group owns 4,000 stores in 10 countries, and the family heirs of Wal-Mart founder Sam Walton rounded out the top 10.

However, executives in other parts of the world were able to capitalise on local growth in particular sectors. Russia's seven billionaires, owners of oil or metals companies, all increased their fortunes or held steady. Canadian french fry magnate Harrison McCain was also up, while Australian wine maker Robert Oately and his family made their debut.

The billionaires club is still dominated by the US and by men, but the group is becoming more diverse. Americans account for 243 people on the list. Europe boasts 121 billionaires. The region with the highest average net worth is the Middle East and Africa, where Prince Al-Waleed bin Talal Alsaud of Saudi Arabia leads the pack with $20bn. And the country with the most billionaire wealth is Sweden, buoyed by Ikea's Ingvar Kamprad.

Forbes compiles its list using share prices and exchange rates. For privately held fortunes, the magazine estimates what companies would be worth if they were public. When possible, the value of art collections, real estate and other assets are included.

Adapted from *The Financial Times, 1.3.2002*

1 What is 'wealth'? (2 marks)
2 Explain the difference between human wealth and non-human wealth. (2 marks)
3 Explain why increasing human wealth is important for economic growth. (4 marks)
4 From the article suggest ways people can accumulate wealth. (4 marks)
5 Suggest three ways in which people can store wealth. (6 marks)
6 How could a government attempt to reduce inequalities in wealth in an economy? (6 marks)
7 Explain why it is difficult to measure the value of wealth. (4 marks)

SUGGESTIONS FOR COURSEWORK

1 Investigate the view that property is the main way to store wealth. Do this by identifying different ways of holding wealth, for example, property, consumer durables, savings, for your family, friends and relatives. Try to explain why different people hold different forms of wealth. You can use graphs and pie charts to illustrate your results.

2 Compare a person on a high income, for example, a pop star or footballer, with a person on a low income, for example, an unemployed person. Explain why there is such a difference in their incomes. Suggest different ways in which this inequality may be reduced and examine the costs and benefits of a redistribution of income towards the poor.

Chapter 18 | The European Economy

The European Economic Community (EEC) was formed in 1958 to provide a common market for trade between France, West Germany, Italy, Belgium, the Netherlands and Luxembourg. A common external tariff was added to the price of goods imported to the EEC from other countries. The EEC members also agreed to a **Common Agricultural Policy (CAP)** which aimed, through guaranteed food prices, to raise and stabilize farmers incomes in the EEC so that they would stay in business. The EEC thought it was important for Europe to produce its own food and reduce its need for imported supplies.

By 1993 twelve countries had joined together to create the European Union (EU), including Spain and Portugal, and by 1995 a further three countries had joined. (The UK had become a member in 1972.) Further expansion of the EU beyond 15 members is planned, including Turkey, Cyprus and a number of the economies of Eastern Europe.

Together the EU member states agreed to establish a **single European Market**. This involves removing restrictions on free trade between their countries, such as frontier checks at customs and the harmonization of indirect taxes such as VAT and excise duties. The single market would also allow freedom of movement of people and capital inside the EU.

EU members also agreed a plan to achieve economic and monetary union (EMU). This involved increased co-ordination of macro-economic policies between EU members, and by 1 January 1999 the introduction of a fixed European **exchange rate mechanism (ERM)** between their national currencies and a single European currency (**the euro**) to replace their national currencies on 1 January 2002. This last stage of the EMU plan also involved the transfer of decision making for monetary policy from each member country to the **European Central Bank**. The ECB now determines interest rates across the EU. However, not all of the 15 members in 1999 adopted this last stage of EMU. The UK and Denmark did not agree to join the ERM and did not replace their national currencies with the euro in January 2002. They also retained control over their individual monetary policies.

Countries in the **eurozone** argued that the single European currency would have great benefits. For example, there would be increased trade because people and businesses in EU countries would no longer have to change their currencies when they visited or traded with other member countries. Increased competition would help lower prices for consumers in the EU because they could now compare prices easily in a single currency in the different EU countries. It was also claimed interest rates across the EU would be lower, to the benefit of borrowers and business investors, because the ECB was committed to keeping inflation low across all member states. In contrast, individual countries with a poor inflation record would have had to keep interest rates higher and for longer to control inflationary pressures.

In contrast, the UK and Denmark argued that the introduction of the single European currency would involve significant changeover costs for businesses – for example, because it would have to print new price lists and train their staff to use the new currency. More importantly, the use of a common interest rate policy across the EU may not be the right policy for all economies. The UK argued that its business cycle was not aligned with the rest of Europe. This means, for example, that the UK might be enjoying low inflation when the rest of Europe is suffering from rising inflationary pressure. As such, the UK could lower interest rates but the ECB would seek to raise interest rates across the EU to combat rising inflation. High interest rates in the UK, if they were not required, would stifle investment and could cause unemployment.

MULTIPLE CHOICE

1 Which of the following is not an objective of the European Union?

  A A single currency
  B Common macroeconomic policies
  C Removal of trade barriers in Europe
  D A common income tax system
  E A common agricultural policy

2 Economic and monetary union in the European Union involves all of the following *except*:

  A A single monetary policy.
  B A single European currency.
  C Zero inflation in Europe.
  D Strict national fiscal policies.
  E A European Central Bank.

3 In 2000 an outbreak of foot and mouth in the UK resulted in a ban on exports of beef from the UK to other members of the European Union. What was the likely effect of this ban on the price of beef in the EU and the UK?

	UK	EU
A	No change	Rise
B	Fall	Rise
C	Rise	Rise
D	Rise	Fall
E	Fall	Fall

4 The common external tariff in the European Union is:

  A A tax charged for changing euros into other currencies.
  B A tax on exports from the UK.
  C A tax on air fares to non-EU countries.
  D A tax on exports to non-EU countries.
  E A tax on imports from non-EU countries.

5 The main advantages claimed for the introduction of the euro in the European Union are:

  1 Reduced exchange rate uncertainty.
  2 Reduced currency transaction costs.
  3 Easier price comparison in different countries.

  A None of the above
  B 1 only
  C 1 and 2 only
  D 2 and 3 only
  E All of the above

6 Economists have calculated the elasticity of demand for a product imported to the European Union from Taiwan is −0.5. What is the most likely effect in the EU of a tariff of 20% added to the price of the imported product?

  A Demand for the product will rise by 10%.
  B The price of the product will rise by more than 20%.
  C The supply of the product will fall by 10%.
  D Demand for the product will fall by 10%.
  E Demand for the product will be unchanged.

DATA RESPONSE 1

The 1992 Maastricht Treaty created a three-stage plan for the introduction of Economic and Monetary Union (EMU) between European Union member states. The three stages are:

- increased co-ordination of macroeconomic policies and completion of the single European market
- a gradual transfer of economic decision making power from national central banks to the European Central Bank
- a fixed exchange rate between EU member currencies, a single European monetary policy and the replacement of national currencies by a Single European Currency (the euro).

Stage 3 of EMU began on 1 January 1999, and the euro eventually replaced national currencies on 1 January 2002.

1 What is a 'fixed exchange rate'?   (2 marks)
2 Explain how monetary policy can be used by a government to influence the level of economic activity in the macroeconomy. (4 marks)
3 Give two economic reasons why the UK and Denmark did not join EMU on 1 January 1999.   (4 marks)
4 Explain two advantages of having a single European currency. (4 marks)

DATA RESPONSE 2

The European Union forms a customs union. A common external tariff is imposed on the price of all imported goods entering the EU from non-member countries. The measure is designed to protect business and jobs inside the EU. Barriers to trade between EU member states are being removed as part of the agreement in 1993 to form a Single European Market.

To avoid the common external tariff many overseas organizations have located operations inside the European Union.

Around 6 per cent of the workforce of the European Union is employed in agriculture. This ranges from over 23 per cent of the workforce in Greece to under 1 per cent in the UK.

Yet around half the annual budget of the European Union is used to guarantee minimum prices for agricultural produce. This has resulted in over production and waste, and consumers in Europe complain about the high prices they must pay for their food.

1 Use demand and supply diagrams to help you describe
  a the effect of the common external tariff on the price and quantity traded of a product imported to the EU from a non-EU country   (4 marks)
  b the effect of introducing a high minimum price in the EU market for an agricultural product.   (4 marks)
2 Explain how the common external tariff is designed to protect businesses and jobs inside EU member countries.   (4 marks)

3 Many farmers have argued reducing agricultural subsidies will force
   many farms to close, but some accept that cutting farm subsidies may
   reduce waste and increase efficiency in agricultural production.
   Explain why both these arguments may be correct.   (8 marks)
4 Suggest two advantages to the European Union of attracting
   businesses from non-EU countries to locate inside the customs
   union.   (4 marks)

SUGGESTIONS FOR COURSEWORK

1 The UK may join the euro zone in the future and transfer decision-
   making on monetary policy to the European Central Bank. Follow the
   debate in the news about the UK replacing the pound by the euro.
   Evaluate the economic arguments used in support of the UK joining in
   full economic and monetary union, and the arguments against. Where
   possible, you should evaluate these arguments against the experience
   of countries that have introduced the euro and full EMU.
2 Investigate the economics of expanding the European Union. What are
   the likely costs and benefits to existing EU member countries and to the
   new member? Contrast and compare the economies of the existing EU
   member states and the new member. For example: what percentage of
   their workforces work in industry and agriculture? what are their rates
   so inflation, unemployment and economic growth? who are their main
   international trading partners and what do they export and import?
3 Consider the economic arguments for and against the introduction of a
   single currency and monetary union in other free trade areas, such as
   COMESA (Common Market for Eastern and Southern Africa), NAFTA
   (North American Free Trade Area) and the Central American Common
   Market. Your work should be informed by the experience of the
   European Union after the introduction of the euro and EMU. From your
   research, suggest whether of not you support the idea and explain the
   reasons for your decision.

   Useful information and data to assist your coursework is published in
   'European Economy'. Visit the European Commission website
   (europa.eu.int/index.htm) for details.

Chapter 19

The Role of Money in an Economy

Money is something we use to buy goods and services. Money is in constant use but we often take it for granted. Yet in the past man existed for many years simply swapping goods and services. This is known as **barter**. However, with the problems of finding a partner to swap with, trying to save perishable goods and trying to agree to a rate of exchange there grew a need for a single commodity everyone would accept in payment for goods and services. Money is a means of exchange, a means of measuring value or pricing commodities, and a store of value; it can also be used in credit arrangements as a means of deferred payment.

Money is used by consumers, firms and governments to buy the services of factors of production, and/or the output of an economy. The market for money consists of all the people and organizations who want to borrow money, and all those people and organizations willing to supply money. The banking system is made up of **financial intermediaries** which act as go-betweens for their customers by attracting savings and making loans. The price of money is the interest rate charged for lending it, or paid to savers.

Notes and coins issued by government, and deposits with financial intermediaries make up the **money supply** in an economy. In modern economies, deposits held in the banking system have become the most important form of money.

Banks have realized that withdrawals of deposits are infrequent and people seldom withdraw all their deposits at once. Banks can lend this idle money to their customers. Cheques are drawn on these loans which must be paid back into the banking system creating more **deposit money**. More loans can then be made. This process is known as **credit creation**.

The banking system consists of commercial banks, merchant banks, finance houses, discount houses and building societies, all specialising in different forms of savings and loans. At the heart of the banking system in an economy is the Central Bank. The Bank of England is the central bank in the UK and a member of the European System of Central Banks. The Governor of the Bank of England is head of the UK Monetary Policy Committee, which meets each month to decide the **base rate** of interest in the UK economy.

MULTIPLE CHOICE

1 Which of the following does not represent a problem associated with barter?

   A The difficulty involved trying to save goods
   B Agreeing on prices acceptable to traders
   C There being no double coincidence of wants
   D Prices of goods being readily available
   E Specialization of production being difficult

2 All the following are important characteristics of a good money *except*:

   A It is durable.
   B It is in unlimited supply.
   C It is generally accepted.
   D It is carried easily.
   E It is divisible into smaller quantities.

3 In which of the following situations would money cease to be a good store of value?

  A Prices of goods and services are falling slowly.
  B High unemployment.
  C Prices of goods and services are rising rapidly.
  D Increased specialization.
  E Prices of goods and services are rising slowly.

4 Which of the following could be termed a commodity money if they are used in exchange for other goods and services?

  A Notes and coins
  B Credit cards
  C Bank deposits
  D Sugar cubes
  E Cheques

5 Which of the following is a function of a Central Bank but not a commercial bank?

  A Holding deposits
  B Making loans
  C Offering financial advice
  D Controlling the money supply
  E Changing foreign currencies

6 Liquidity is defined as:

  A The ability to convert paper money into gold.
  B The ability to save.
  C The ability to convert cash into goods and services.
  D The ability to convert assets into cash.
  E The ability to accumulate wealth.

7 In general the supply of money in a modern economy is best defined as:

  A Notes issued by the Central Bank.
  B Coins, notes and bank deposits.
  C All items of legal tender.
  D Coins, notes and deposits with financial institutions.
  E Notes and coins.

8 Building Societies obtain their funds from:

  A Buying and selling property.
  B Government.
  C Savers.
  D Selling shares on a stock exchange.
  E Borrowing from commercial banks.

9 Which of the following assets is the most liquid?

  A A 90-day savings account
  B The value of a life insurance policy
  C Gold jewelry
  D Notes and coins
  E A 10-year government bond

10 Finance houses specialize in:

  A Banking services for businesses.
  B Helping consumers to buy goods on credit.
  C Lending money for hire purchase.
  D Keeping money safely for customers.
  E Helping customers make and receive payment.

Look at the pictures below.

 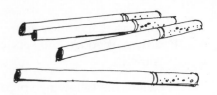

1 Which of the items above could be used in a barter
  exchange? (4 marks)
2 Why did barter prove so difficult? (4 marks)
3 The introduction of money can overcome the problems of
  barter, but which of the above items could act as a 'good' money?
  Consider each one in turn and explain your answers. (10 marks)
4 What three functions must your 'good' money perform? (6 marks)
5 Many people hold liquid assets which can be changed back
  into cash when they need it. Give three examples of
  widely-held liquid assets. (6 marks)
6 What effect will price inflation have on the value of money
  over time? (4 marks)

The table below presents the interest rates offered by a particular commercial bank on a selection of different deposit accounts.

Account	Conditions	Interest rate % (annual equivalent rate)
Flexi-saver (instant access)	Minimum deposit £1 No withdrawal notice	2.00%
90-day access	Minimum deposit £100 90 days withdrawal notice required or loss of interest	3.65%
5-year tax-free account	Minimum deposit £3 000 Tax-free if kept for 5 years	4.20%
One-year bond	Minimum deposit £10 000 Fixed 1-year term	4.65%

1   What is a deposit account? (2 marks)
2   Suggest reasons for banks offering interest to people to save money in a deposit account. (4 marks)
3   Explain why the rate of interest on the one year bond is higher than the interest rate available to savers with instant access to their savings. (4 marks)
4   The bank has recently introduced 'home banking' which allows customers to check their accounts and make payments using the internet. What are the likely benefits to the bank of Internet banking? (4 marks)
5   The bank uses the money saved in its deposit accounts to make loans. Explain how this can increase the money supply in the economy. (4 marks)
6   Explain why the bank is likely to charge a higher rate of interest for a five year loan for £10 000 to a new business start-up than a 3-year loan for £25 000 to an established and well-known business. (6 marks)
7   The bank has also recently issued a low-interest credit card. Discuss how the widespread availability of credit cards may affect the level of consumer spending in an economy, business investment, price inflation, and the balance of trade. (6 marks)

The euro comes into its own

The euro becomes sole legal tender in the eurozone , capping an extraordinarily smooth changeover

By the end of tomorrow, the last of the eurozone's old national currencies will become obsolete, and the euro will be the only legal tender throughout the area.

That this historic event will pass largely unnoticed by the 12-nation eurozone's 300 million citizens testifies to the efficiency with which the changeover has been managed.

For the European Central Bank, it gives rise to confidence that the exercise can be repeated just as smoothly, and rapidly, if and when the euro is introduced in other existing and future member states.

Adapted from *The Financial Times, 27.2.2002*

1　List four functions euro notes and coins should perform.　(4 marks)
2　Explain how consumer price inflation in Europe may affect these functions.　(4 marks)
3　Describe two methods, other than cheques and credit cards, that European banks can provide to help their customers make payments in euros.　(4 marks)
4　Central banks are responsible for the issue of euro notes and coins. Describe two other functions central banks have.　(4 marks)
5　Explain why the European Central Bank may restrict the supply of money in the European economy to raise interest rates during a period of rising price inflation.　(6 marks)

SUGGESTIONS FOR COURSEWORK

1　Collect information from the financial press on countertrade between countries, that is, barter. Analyse carefully the types of commodities exchanged and the reasons for this.
2　Using information collected from the financial press and local banks compare and contrast the various ways banks compete for people's and firms' deposits.
3　Imagine all present-day forms of money disappear overnight. Compare and contrast the use of various commodities as a form of money to replace the old systems.
4　Investigate the introduction of new technology and banking methods by commercial banks. Why are these changes taking place? Analyse the effects these changes could have on domestic economic activity and international trade.

The population of the world today is approximately 6 billion people and is growing quickly.

In 1798 Thomas Malthus predicted that population would outgrow the number of resources in the world – that is, there would be overpopulation and this would result in starvation. However, this has not yet happened because of better technology and investment which has resulted in economic growth.

In the less developed world, Malthus may still be proved right as high population growth threatens to outstrip the ability of these countries to produce enough goods and services.

It is possible to measure the effect of population on living standards using the **dependency ratio**. The dependency ratio for a country can be found by dividing the total population by the number of people in work. For example, in the UK there are roughly 60 million people. Of these, 27 million people are in paid employment and so must produce the goods and services needed to support themselves and the remaining 33 million dependents (made up of children, unemployed, sick and disabled). Using this method the UK has a dependency ratio of 2.22, meaning that every working person must support, on average, 2.22 dependents, including themselves.

There are three ways in which a country's population may increase:
1 The number of births rise.
2 The number of deaths fall.
3 More people come to live in a country (immigration) than there are people leaving the country (emigration).

The **regional distribution of population** refers to where people live. In the UK, most people live in seven conurbations, which consist of towns that have gradually grown together to form large cities.

The **age distribution of population** refers to the number of people in each age group. With falling birth and death rates in the UK the average age of the population has increased. The UK is experiencing an ageing population.

The **sex distribution of population** refers to the number of males compared to females in the population. Although there is a higher male birth rate than female birth rate in the UK, the number of females (50.1% in 1999) outnumbers the number of males (49.2% in 1999) because females tend to live longer than males.

The **occupational distribution of population** refers to the types of jobs that people do. Over 75% of people work in the service or tertiary industry in the UK; 21% of people are employed in manufacturing, or secondary industry; and 4% in agriculture and other primary industries.

The **optimum** population of a country is that size of population which given the existing stock of land, labour and capital could produce the maximum amount of output per head.

MULTIPLE CHOICE

1 Which of the following countries has a high population growth rate?

 A France
 B Denmark
 C Malawi
 D Austria
 E Canada

2 What is meant by overpopulation?

 A Too many people to an area of land
 B High population density
 C Scare resources
 D Too many people and not enough resources
 E High population growth

3 What is meant by the dependency ratio of a country?

 A The number of people over 16 years of age compared to the total population
 B The number of dependent relatives in the total population
 C The number of children compared to the adult population
 D The number of people working compared to the total population
 E The number of old people compared to the total population

4 Which of the following factors is likely to cause an increase in the birth rate in a country?

 A Contraceptives being freely supplied
 B An increase in living standards
 C More education
 D Earlier marriages
 E More female employment

5 Death rates are likely to fall if:

 A Housing conditions are improved.
 B More people smoke.
 C Health care deteriorates.
 D People's diets become less healthy.
 E The number of cars increases.

6 The working population of a country includes all of the following except:
 1 Students over the age of 18.
 2 The self-employed.
 3 The unemployed.

 A 1 only
 B 2 only
 C 3 only
 D 1 and 2
 E All of them

7 The population in a country will increase if:
 1 There is more emigration.
 2 Death rates rise.
 3 Birth rates rise.

 A 1 only
 B 2 only
 C 3 only
 D 1 and 2
 E All of them

8 Which of the following describes the present UK population?
 1 There are more females than males.
 2 Population growth is low.
 3 The average age is rising.

 A 1 only
 B 2 only
 C 3 only
 D 1 and 2
 E All of them

Population change

United Kingdom   Thousands

	Population at start of period	Annual averages				
		Live births	Deaths	Net natural change	Net migration and other	Overall change
Census enumerated						
1901–1911	38 237	1091	624	467	−82	385
1911–1921	42 082	975	689	286	−92	194
1921–1931	44 027	824	555	268	−67	201
1931–1951	46 038	785	598	188	25	213
Mid-year estimates						
1951–1961	50 287	839	593	246	12	258
1961–1971	52 807	962	638	324	−14	310
1971–1981	55 928	736	666	69	−27	42
1981–1991	56 357	757	655	103	43	146
1991–1999	57 814	744	637	107	104	211
Mid-year projections						
1999–2001	59 501	716	627	88	140	228
2001–2011	59 954	701	614	87	95	182
2011–2021	61 773	712	620	92	95	187

Office of National Statistics, Social Trends 2001

1 From the table describe how the total UK population has
   changed over time and is projected to change in the future.   (2 marks)
2 Identify and describe three key trends from the table that
   explain UK population change over time.   (6 marks)
3 Suggest two factors that can explain the change over time in
   live births each year in the UK.   (4 marks)
4 Given the information on births and deaths in the table, how
   do you think the average age of the UK population has
   changed since 1901?   (2 marks)
5 Explain two possible consequences of the change in the average
   age of the UK population (as you have described in response
   to question 4 above) on the UK economy.   (4 marks)

The charts below show the approximate percentage of working people employed in the three different sectors of the economies of the United Kingdom and Brazil in 2001.

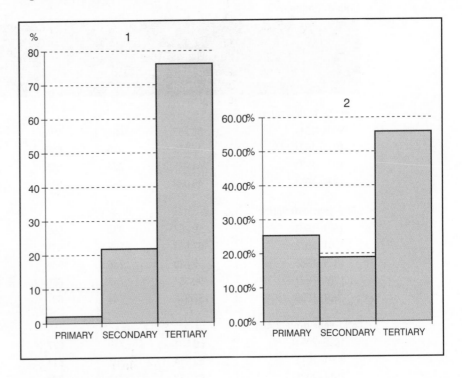

1 Define a primary industry and give two examples. (4 marks)

2 a What is the difference between a secondary and a tertiary industry? (2 marks)

  b Give two examples of each. (4 marks)

3 Which chart, 1 or 2, do you think best represents:

  a The United Kingdom?

  b Brazil? (2 marks)

4 How would you expect the chart to look for the United Kingdom and Brazil in 20 years' time. Explain your answer. (6 marks)

5 How are the changing patterns you discussed in question 4 likely to affect the regional distribution of population in the United Kingdom and Brazil? (2 marks)

6 Many females in the United Kingdom are finding employment in the tertiary sector of the economy.

  a How could this affect UK birth rates?

  b Suggest three other factors that have caused a change in the birth rate in the United Kingdom over the last 100 years. (8 marks)

THE FUTURE'S BRIGHT, THE FUTURE'S GREY

It will be a grey-haired world. There will be fewer Chinese, Europeans and Japanese, and more Africans, Indians and Americans. And at last, the planet will be getting a little less crowded. In the most sophisticated forecast so far of global population over the next hundred years, scientists say that by the end of the century, it will almost certainly be falling.

A team at Austria's International Institute for Applied Systems Analysis (IIASA) says the world population, now a little over 6bn, is likely to peak at about 9bn in 70 years time. By 2100, it will have gone down to 8.4bn, and will keep falling.

Dr Lutz, head of the research project, warned that the price to be paid for a shrinking world population was an increase in the number of elderly people in the world.

Key predictions from the global population forecast
- The world's population is likely to peak at 9bn in 2070. By 2100, it will be 8.4bn.
- North America (the US and Canada) will be one of only two regions in the world with a population still growing in 2100. The other expanding region will be Latin America
- Despite disease, war and hunger, the population of Africa will grow from 784m today to 1.6bn in 2050.

By 2100 it will be 1.8bn, although it will have begun to decline. By the end of the century more than a fifth of Africans will be over 60, more than in western Europe today.
- The China region (China and Hong Kong together with five smaller neighbouring nations) will see its population shrink significantly by 2100, from 1.4bn to 1.25bn. Because of its education programme, by 2020, when China is reaching its population peak of about 1.6bn, it will have more well-educated people than Europe and North America combined.
- India will overtake China as the world's most populous nation by 2020.
- Europe – including Turkey and the former Soviet Union west of the Urals – will see its population fall from 813 m now to 607 m in 2100: from 13% of the world's population to just 7%. Eastern countries such as Russia have already seen their populations fall; western Europe's is likely to peak in the next few decades.
- One 10th of the world's population is over 60. By 2100, that proportion will have risen to one-third.
- In 1950, there were thought to be three times as many Europeans as Africans. By 2100, the proportions will be reversed.

Adapted from *The Guardian, 2.8.2001*

1 Describe the future population trends, both globally and for different regions/countries, as described in the above article. (10 marks)
2 Use your knowledge of economics to suggest how the forecast changes in the level and distribution of the world's population may affect the availability and allocation of resources between different parts of the world and between different markets. (15 marks)

SUGGESTIONS FOR COURSEWORK

1 Analyse the effects of an increase in population on the demand for the services provided by your local authority or regional government.

2 Investigate trends in the movements of population in the United Kingdom or in your own country. Concentrate especially on the movement of people between different regions and between major cities and towns to/from rural areas. Display this information using bar graphs and pie charts, etc. Can you offer any explanation for your findings. What are the likely effects of these movements on consumers, producers and citizens in these different areas?

The following useful websites can provide data on population for your coursework:

- UK Office for National Statistics (www.statistics.gov.uk)
- US Population Bureau (www.prb.org)
- United Nations (www.un.org/esa)